MW01036970

Bridging the
GREAT DIVIDE

Reuniting Word and Spirit

ROB MCCORKLE
Foreword by Daniel Ketchum

PRESS

Copyright © 2015 by Rob McCorkle

Bridging the Great Divide
Reuniting Word and Spirit
by Rob McCorkle

Printed in the United States of America.

ISBN 9781498440554

All rights reserved solely by the author. The author guarantees all contents are original and do not infringe upon the legal rights of any other person or work. No part of this book may be reproduced in any form without the permission of the author. The views expressed in this book are not necessarily those of the publisher.

Unless otherwise indicated, Scripture quotations taken from the New King James Version (NKJV). Copyright © 1982 by Thomas Nelson, Inc. Used by permission. All rights reserved.

www.xulonpress.com

Acknowledgments

To Randy Clark—In the spring of 2008, he prayed that Cindy and I would be used to re-dig the wells in the Holiness movement; his prophetic words have come true. He taught me to value the importance of an impartation. I'm also grateful for his invitation to pursue a Doctor of Ministry degree, where I united with a cohort of eighteen people from different parts of our world. I came to appreciate, through our experiences together, the passion and faith of each person in my group and will cherish our friendship for a lifetime.

To my doctoral mentors—Gary Greig, who helped me see Word and Spirit almost everywhere in the Bible, Jon Ruthven, who taught me the importance of living a true biblical emphasis, and Andrew Park, who modeled the humility of Jesus Christ.

To my close friends who live in intimacy with Christ in such a manner that it results in a supernatural lifestyle—Dan and Debbie Bohi, Chad and Melissa Cline, Ron and Kathy Frizzell, Corey and Beth Ann Jones, Daniel and Carol Ketchum, Bryan and Dawn McConnell, Craig and Connie Rench, and Kevin and Marsha Seymour.

To my Oasis group, a place where rest and laughter are normal—Rob and Mary Farrell, Roger and Terri Hamilton, Dan and Nancy Lembke, Stan and Barb Mink, and Allan and Karen Rasnake.

To my church, Crossroads Community Church—A church that encouraged me to take a sabbatical and then experienced and embraced the fruit of my encounter.

To my faithful prayer partners—Jim and Tami Dixon, who avert much disaster over our ministry because of their intercession.

To Rhonda Hughey—For her suggestions for the title of this book and more importantly her inspirational stories of desperate, hungry people.

To my editor—Karen Stout, who made sense of my notes.

To my sons and their spouses—Wes and Jordan (and grandson, Archer) and Jesse and Natalie. My ceiling will be their floor as they continue in ministry.

To Cindy—My wife and best friend, who personifies the Word and the Spirit.

Endorsements

———⟨𝓋𝓋⟩———

In his book, Rob McCorkle states that he appreciates "the attempts that have been made in bringing purity and power together, but it is not enough for the two concepts to simply abide together or hold hands as friends. The divorce must end and a remarriage must be reestablished. We must experience a one-flesh union with purity and power as observed in the Wesleyan crusades." This book spells out what that remarriage would look like and is a must read for those in the Methodist, Charismatic, and Pentecostal traditions. His chapter on "Discipleship in the Supernatural" is especially helpful.

Dr. Frank Billman
Director of Equipping Ministries at Aldersgate Renewal Ministries
Dean of the Methodist School for Supernatural Ministries
D. Min Mentor for Supernatural Ministries at
United Theological Seminary

I'm so grateful for Rob's book, giving language to the things that I have learned in the Spirit these last six years as I've traveled the country preaching the gospel. This book has strengthened and encouraged my faith to never shrink back in proclaiming the reality of His kingdom, and wanting to see it break into our world through our obedient lives of faith. I would encourage every believer to read this book if you're hungry for a deeper, more intimate relationship with Jesus.

Dan Bohi
Itinerant Speaker
Dan Bohi Ministry

Rob McCorkle's book, *Bridging the Great Divide: Reuniting Word and Spirit,* is a great book, a necessary book, a book for our time. I encourage every Christian, every pastor, to buy and read it. Rob has written it with the favor of God and the wind of the Spirit behind him. He asks the right questions! He provides good answers to those questions. He is passionate for His triune God and for the Bride of Christ. He does not bring a sledge hammer to operate on a sick church, but a surgeon's scalpel. I am proud of his book, its passion, its focus, its ability to heal the *great divide,* and its solid biblical and theological emphasis, as well as its value for the experiential, as well. I plan to carry it in our "on-the-road bookstore" for our schools of Revival, as well as our four different schools of healing and impartation.

Dr. Randy Clark
Overseer of the Apostolic Network of Global Awakening

Dr. Rob McCorkle's book, *Bridging the Great Divide,* has skillfully described the biblical and historical foundations for God's desire to restore the threefold emphasis of Word, Spirit, and Holiness to not only the Church of the Nazarene and the denominations stemming from the Wesleyan Holiness movement, but to the whole Body of Christ today. The Lord intends this threefold-cord emphasis to be sown back into the whole Body of Christ today so we can finish strong in the intensifying Kingdom warfare of the Last Days and bring in the greatest harvest of souls the planet has ever witnessed. Through the threefold emphasis on Word, Spirit, and Holiness, the Lord wants to make us His Body to be a seat for His glory in the Last Days—a fit temple for His presence, to reach and touch all nations with the transforming power of the gospel of the Kingdom.

Dr. Gary S. Greig
Near Eastern Languages and Civilizations
The University of Chicago
Vice President of Biblical Content, Gospel Light Publications
Adjunct faculty, United Theological Seminary

God has truly given Rob McCorkle a prophetic voice to call the church back to the ancient path of holiness. To be clear, what God has given Rob is so much more than a message on paper. In fact, Rob embodies what he preaches, which is really the biblical, New Testament emphasis on the fusion of purity (holiness of heart) and power (demonstrations and signs of the Spirit). In other words, signs and wonders are evident and follow what Rob shares, witnesses to, and proclaims. God knows how desperately we need prophets in this generation, and in my opinion, Dr. Rob McCorkle is one of those prophetic voices. We do well to hear and heed what God is saying through this man of God.

Pastor Corey Jones
Fort Worth, TX
Church of the Nazarene

In this study, Dr. Rob McCorkle has sought to point out that there is a great divorce in the contemporary Holiness movements between being and action, or more precisely, purity and power, Word and Spirit. It seems to me that both (the non-Pentecostal holiness movement and the Pentecostal/Charismatic movement) belief systems and practices have been compromised by a theological shift. The solution that Dr. McCorkle advances is profound and winsome; both movements would do well to adopt a lifestyle of intimacy with Christ in purity and knowledge, and to activate a God who really acts by drawing upon power to live in the realm of the supernatural. This is a great challenge that merits consideration and adoption.

Dr. Don Owens
General Superintendent Emeritus
Church of the Nazarene

Our Lord, through Rob McCorkle and others like him, seems to be placing revival squarely in the lap of the U.S. Holiness movement. The question: will we receive and respond to His truth, or rationalize and reject? Rob is not fundamentally calling us to either holiness or healing, but to the Holy One who brings both, and with holiness and healing will come massive revival and evangelism.

Hal Perkins
Itinerant Speaker
Founder of Heart Walk Ministries

Rob McCorkle has written a classic! He has powerfully and dynamically fused together the two great wings of the Holiness/Charismatic movements into God's original divine design: Word and Spirit, purity and power. Too long has the "great divide" separated the people of the Holy Spirit. Rob masterfully demonstrates from Scripture and from church history that we desperately need both the doctrine (Word of God/ Purity) and the *dunamis* (Spirit/Power). Using impeccable logic, humor, history, and passion, he reveals how we got to where we are, and then he weaves together what never should have been divided. Rob writes what I have believed and taught for decades—but he says it much better than I ever could have! If you care about holiness like God does and if you care about walking in the power that God intended each believer to operate in, then you need to read and re-read this mighty work.

Pastor Craig W. Rench
Anaheim, CA
Church of the Nazarene
Author: *The Master's Plan*

Contents

———ᔕᔕᔕ———

Foreword

—◦⁄⁄⁄◦—

R ob McCorkle is one of God's mighty men like King
David's mighty men in 2 Samuel 23: valiant victors,
fearless overcomers, exploit-experienced, cherished champions, and faithful servants.

I first met and heard Rob preach at a Purity and Power
Conference with Dan Bohi, hosted by Pastor Lenny Wisehart.
For seven years, I have admired Rob's biblical integrity,
contagious spirit, humble authority, and prophetic passion
at church altars, in conferences with Pastor Corey Jones, in
weeklong prayer gatherings at the Nazarene Global Ministry
Center, and over dinner several times. One night following
dinner in our home, my wife Carol and I asked Rob and
Cindy McCorkle and Ron and Kathy Frizzell to place their
hands on us and pray that God would pour His Spirit through
our lives with fresh impartation for others. They did. He has.

Rob answered God's call to ministry in 1982 and began
preaching within months. He completed a BA at Mount
Vernon Nazarene University in Ohio. Later he met and married Cindy. They discipled two sons, Wes and Jess, who are
both married and are in the ministry. Rob completed a Master
of Divinity at Nazarene Theological Seminary in 1990. In
2013, he earned a Doctor of Ministry at United Theological
Seminary. At both seminaries, Rob studied the historic
Christian faith, as well as cultivation of holiness and renewal

of the Church. He pursued life-changing power in Holy Spirit through holy hearts and lives that transform persons around the world by making disciple makers as Jesus intended. He focused on the integrated work of the Word and Holy Spirit as renewal—individual, congregational, and global—that can be seen, heard, felt, and reproduced. He has become a leader in church renewal.

The major turning point in Rob's life came in 2007. Encouraged by his district superintendent, he took a seven-week sabbatical. During that time, Rob encountered the manifest presence of God, whose glory for several days washed, revived, and renewed his heart. When Rob returned to pastor his people, God poured out on them the revelation that revival can be lived every day; they experienced sanctifications, healings, miracles, and deliverances. They embraced the fusion of purity and power.

In 2008, God called Rob to continue pastoring while speaking and writing to re-dig the wells in the Holiness movement. He founded Fire School Ministries to awaken churches to the message of purity and power and to function in the Word and the Spirit. This lifestyle replicates the life of Jesus and the believers in the book of Acts. Rob proclaims the Word and functions with anointing in the Spirit. His intent during every church gathering and conference is that each person encounters the living God. He believes deeply that if persons depart without this encounter, they merely become more religious. He asserts God's intent to draw each of us closer to Himself, to His manifest presence in Jesus, and to His Spirit.

Rob has published other resources, which have contributed to the timely import and riveting essence of *Bridging the Great Divide*. He has navigated a biblical and theological field of land mines, and he has done it with grace, sensitivity, courage, and exegetical acumen, helping to navigate the way for all of us. Rob is uniquely qualified for this challenge. First, more than anything, he is a lover of God, desiring to please Him more than to promote a people or a cause. Second, he is a man of prayer and power, just as eager to pour out compassion and intercession as he is to declare God's healing and wholeness over disease and God's authority over demons. Third, as a practical theologian, he is meticulous in research, persuasive in declaration, and balanced in personal application. Fourth, as a careful student of Scripture and Spirit, he avoids common interpretive errors, relies on scholarly as well as revelatory resources, and engages in transformative acts.

Rob advocates for the proclamation of the Word in holiness and heart purity, so that pastors, leaders, and laypeople experience the deep, cleansing work of God in tandem with the supernatural power of the Spirit demonstrated in extraordinary miracles. He grieves over churches and persons who downplay the power of Holy Spirit. He is fervent for the fusion of Word and Spirit to empower especially non-Pentecostal holiness churches. He proposes a lifestyle of intimacy with Christ in which each of us activates the Word and reproduces a lifestyle that is natural in the *super*natural.

I commend to you wholeheartedly Rob's character (purity and power) in Christ and the ways he models and re-presents the Word and Holy Spirit across the Body of Messiah. As you read this book with a prayerful, open mind and healthy courage, God can change your life and add your name to the list of mighty ones: valiant victors, fearless overcomers, exploit-experienced, cherished champions, and faithful servants.

Daniel D. Ketchum, PhD
Servant of Yeshua the Messiah
Daily in the Word and Spirit
Jerusalem, Israel

Introduction

What happens when approximately one thousand people, fifty pastors, and eighteen different denominations gather in one place, and the presence of God moves in a mighty way? You encounter an experience that reveals the true identity of the bride of Christ. My friend Dan Bohi and I experienced this in Joplin, Missouri, during a conference that we led, and it was a life-altering event; we witnessed many miracles that evening, such as tumors disappearing, marriages being restored, lust being confessed and purged, backs being healed, sinners being saved, believers being sanctified, and the restoration of God's glory upon all who were present.

As I reflected upon this gathering, there were no dividing walls between the pastors or churches, no distinctions between our denominational titles, and no barriers to hinder the move of God. We simply were God's people doing God's business. As we taught and ministered, we witnessed the culmination of the Word and the Spirit. Holiness and heart purity were being proclaimed from the Word where pastors, leaders, and laypeople experienced the deep, cleansing work of God in tandem with the supernatural power of the Spirit demonstrated in extraordinary miracles and breakthroughs.

The unity of Word and Spirit that we witnessed that night is the pattern that Jesus initiated as we read the pages of the New Testament. Jesus' inaugural message in Luke 4:18 began when He declared that the Holy Spirit rested upon Him for two central reasons. First, Jesus said that the Holy Spirit was upon Him to *preach* the Word: the declaration of deliverance, healing, restoration, and salvation. Second, the Holy Spirit was going to enable Him to bring the *recovery* of sight to the blind, which is the miraculous power of God displayed by the Spirit.[1] This two-fold punch of preaching the Word and performing miraculous deeds characterized everything that Jesus did. The necessity to function in Word and Spirit is what spurred Jesus' rebuke to the Sadducees when He said to them, "You are mistaken, not knowing the Scriptures nor the power of God" (Matt. 22:29). Jesus ministered the Word, and He displayed supernatural power by the Spirit. This style of ministry was described by Luke in his prologue in Acts, when he described the things he saw Jesus *do* and *teach*.

The challenge, however, for the Church of today, for you and for me, is not to merely accept that Jesus ministered in Word and Spirit, but to accept the fact that we should replicate Him in this particular lifestyle as we are commanded to do (John 14:12). I truly believe that we have deviated from Jesus' style of ministry and the unity of Word and Spirit. How did this occur? I believe cessationism (the belief that miraculous spiritual gifts are no longer necessary), traditional Christian education built on incorrect theological premises, and discipleship programs that divorce the Word and the Spirit (purity and power) are the sources of erosion. The objective of this book is to examine these three reasons and present some biblical, historical, and theological responses. The greater objective of this book is to propose a lifestyle of intimacy with Christ where we learn to activate the Word like Him and to encourage us to live naturally in the *super*natural.

Some of the content of this book has been adapted from the dissertation that I completed in December 2013. My project, which included teaching supernatural gifts to Nazarene participants, was a culmination of my heart and ministry. Obtaining a doctorate was an incredible process and event, but watching people become activated to the Word and the Spirit was a thrill of a lifetime and continues to be a much greater blessing to me. This book distills the research and experiences of my ministry project and provides what I believe to be the necessary ingredients for an effective spiritual life inside and outside the church walls.

My hope is that as you read each page you sense the great concern that grips my heart for the Holiness movement within the United States. My whole life has been spent in the Nazarene church, and I have been blessed by the ministry of many servants of the Lord who have invested time to teach and equip me. I am forever grateful and humbled by their lives. While the context for my dissertation focused on the Church of the Nazarene, I believe that all churches within the Holiness movement (including Pentecostal and Charismatic churches) will benefit from this book. That being said, I believe the non-Pentecostal churches in the Holiness movement, which is my immediate concern, have downplayed the power of the Holy Spirit—especially in terms of replicating Jesus in supernatural ways. As you will read in the pages that follow, we've made a grave error by separating the Word and the Spirit. It's the prayer of my heart, and the intention of this book, to see the fusion of Word and Spirit.

Chapter One

How It Began for Me

———∾∿∾———

I tried the best I could to avoid that voice. It started around the age of twelve—that still, small voice of the Lord calling me into the ministry. But the thought of preaching terrified me, so instead of accepting the call from God, I ran away from that voice and into rebellion. The events of my life from the age of twelve to the age of twenty are blurred. The memories that I have are colored with sorrow and regret, largely because of the decisions that I was making at the time.

Barely scraping through high school, my plan was to leave home and join the Air Force because I desired, like most teenagers, to be as far away from my parents as possible. Although I loved them dearly and they daily modeled true Christianity, their desires for me conflicted with my desires to live a lifestyle void of Christ. The wisdom of my father prevailed, however, when he cautioned me about entering the military just so that I could "do my own thing." With much urging, he convinced me to spend one year at a Christian college. So in the fall of 1981, I enrolled into Mount Vernon Nazarene University.

During the fall of my first semester, I reluctantly attended a student revival. It was during one of the evening services that Christ captured me. To describe my spiritual conversion as an ambush would not adequately describe what I felt. Truly, I was overtaken by God's grace for the first time in my life. Growing up in church, I saw many people respond to invitations to receive Christ. My memory is chock-full of youth camps where many students came forward and made emotional commitments to God. But that fall evening was life altering because I experienced a personal side of God that, for me, was altogether new. On that night, I was forgiven and redeemed by God's grace, and He gave me the ability to make a true difference with my life.

That following summer, I attended a camp in St. Marys, Ohio, where the evening speaker spoke passionately about going into deeper spiritual waters. His message was a clear call to surrender one's life to God in total consecration, a reckless abandonment to God to be sanctified wholly. I feared this subject matter because deep within my spirit, I sensed that God would again resurrect the call to full-time ministry. Yet just months before, I had been gloriously redeemed from a life of sin and believed God had more planned for my life. That night I surrendered my life in faith before God with no conditions, no reservations, and no apprehensions. God did begin speaking to me about preaching; however, this time I had no other response than full obedience.

In the years following I was married, graduated from college, and moved to Kansas City, Kansas, where I enrolled in Nazarene Theological Seminary to pursue a master's of divinity degree. After graduating from seminary and spending seven years in the pastorate, we moved to Columbus, Ohio, to plant a church. In November 1997, a small group launched Crossroads Community Church (Nazarene) in a high school auditorium on the southeast side of Columbus. We were completely unprepared for the one hundred and eighty-six people who walked into the school the morning of our first service. It seemed like we were sailing our maiden voyage with minimal construction completed on our vessel. During those first few years, we found that we had many holes and leaks in our structure, and seemingly our only opportunity to patch them was during the few hours that we met in the rented school building as we weekly set up and tore down our church. Near the end of our seventh year in the high school, another problem emerged; I was becoming spiritually exhausted. I was investing many hours trying to build this young congregation, but to no avail. As people came in through the front door, others left through the back. I felt powerless to stop the hemorrhaging, and worse still, I was struggling to clearly hear the voice of God. Rather than take the time to repair the spiritual breach in my personal life, I simply pressed on doing ministry.

The paradigm of our church was modeled after Willow Creek Community Church in Chicago. All of our services were designed to be seeker friendly. This church model required many weekly man-hours of planning, and the focus of our services was to have an attractive production as opposed to having an experience filled with the presence of God. I can't blame that intent on Willow Creek, but my focus was to become the best ninety-minute show in town; and our services were just that. However, the fallout of that kind of paradigm can be the absence of God's Spirit, a superficial church, and little spiritual transformation in people's lives.

The day of reckoning came after an especially long weekend. We had just completed a Christmas play that had required months of hard work and preparation from twenty-five cast members and other stage members. The multiple performances had packed the high school auditorium with close to four hundred people that particular weekend. After the last performance and before I turned out the lights, I found myself sitting alone on the stage thumbing through the response cards from the final performance. Not a single person had received salvation that entire weekend as a result of the hours of hard work we had dedicated to this Christmas play. Beyond that, I cannot honestly tell you that anyone really sensed the manifest presence of God. Had all of the hard work been in vain, I thought.

I began to think about all the church-growth programs we had attempted in the past seven years, twenty-one days of this program or forty days of that, and to be honest, we had very little to show for it. I had gone to every church-growth seminar I knew of and attempted to implement every innovative idea, but there was no real, lasting change in people's lives. We spent hours of preparation for our services each weekend, but in the final analysis, we were simply filling seats rather than seeing lives touched by the power of God. That morning, while sitting on an empty stage, I sensed the voice of the Lord asking me, "Have you ever thought of trying it My way?" Yet I continued on the same path, and it was two more years before I would sense the voice of the Lord speaking to me again.

By the fall of 2006, I was completely spent. I realized something had broken inside my heart, and nothing was fixing it. I did not desire a life of sin; I just had no joy! I had tried going to counseling but to no avail. The emptiness that I felt in my heart only seemed to increase; my anger toward God and my frustration with ministry only intensified. Besides my family's awareness of what I was going through, I shared my condition with two senior leaders at our church and my district superintendent.They recommended that I take a seven-week sabbatical before making any decision about the church or my ministry. With their counsel in mind, I informed my church board that I was going to leave for seven weeks, beginning in January of 2007.

One of the most sobering moments of my life came for me in December of 2006, one week before my departure. I sat humbly before my leaders at the church and informed them that I was at the helm of a ship but had absolutely no idea where to steer the vessel. I was a man with no revelation, no vision from God; and not only were people perishing, but I was lost. All of my education, all of the seminars and notebooks, all of the church-growth books and slick programs meant very little to me at that moment. Life is in the voice of God, and I was dying from the absence of it. I put my head on the table and wept; I had very little hope that I would ever return to this church or the ministry again.

I crawled out of Columbus two weeks into my sabbatical and buried myself for a few weeks at a cottage in Summersville, West Virginia. Over the years, I had read accounts of people experiencing encounters with God in times of desperation. Some have seen fire, while others have had visions or fell to the ground trembling in His presence, and still others heard the audible voice of God; even Moses saw a burning bush and Balaam heard a talking donkey, but to be brutally honest, I did not have any expectations of encountering God. In retrospect, I was just desperate. It had been nearly two years since hearing His voice, so I was not expecting what was about to happen. But in a unique, profound, and powerful manner, the glory of God descended upon me. For several days I was overcome by the manifest presence of God; it was real, it was palpable, and it forever altered my life.

One particular morning, I realized for the first time in my life that God truly loved me in spite of how I had loved Him. God washed over me; He baptized me in His love, and my ice-cold anger and cynicism melted away. Overcome by the love of God, I lay on the floor weeping uncontrollably as layers of insecurity, pride, performance, and image-managing were stripped away. For the first time in my adult life I realized there was a difference between working *for* God and working *from* Him. During those days, I gained a revelation that I had been living like the elder brother in the story of the Prodigal son told by Jesus in Luke 15. I had spent my entire Christian experience *slaving* for the Father, doing all of the right things but never really knowing Him as "Papa" (Rom. 8:15). Beyond that, like the elder brother, I had no idea that my Father had already given me the farm (Luke 15:31). I didn't realize that I had a rich spiritual inheritance and as a result, I had been living my life asking why I hadn't been given even a single calf. I was living like a spiritual orphan, and my Christian experience was more like that of a pauper than a prince. Because I was serving God like a slave, I didn't have any idea of the Master's business, and I had no sense of intimacy with God prior to this time (John 15:15).

Those weeks alone in Summersville imprinted a Spirit of revelation upon my heart. Not only did I hear the voice of God, but I experienced an intimacy in the chamber room with Him that left me speechless at times. Since those days of intense encounters with God, nothing has ever appealed more to me than being in the manifest presence of God and living daily in His presence. My only desire now is to do ministry out of intimacy *with* Christ, not *for* Christ. Realizing that life is in His voice, I only want to be close enough to hear Him speak every moment. I have been wrecked, in a good sense, and it will take a lifetime to recover.

God had renewed my calling to remain at Crossroads, but I knew our paradigm would require a shift. No longer would we structure services for seekers; rather, we would structure them for the presence of God. My thoughts shifted from the comfort of seekers to the pleasure of God. I realized that God was more interested in seeing seekers transformed than I was, and He was certainly more capable of designing a service to accomplish that goal. All He asked of us was to create an environment for the habitation of His glory and then to watch as He would touch people's lives. My messages changed, our music transitioned, and our entire church went from being a performance-based church to a presence-based church. Crossroads became a place where people started having encounters with God, much like I did during my sabbatical.

The first year of the new paradigm shift, our church experienced exponential encounters with God. We saw miracles of every kind, and the manifestation of the spiritual gifts that

Paul wrote about in 1 Corinthians 12 came alive. People actually were healed of diseases and chronic illnesses when we prayed for them, and I realized that I witnessed more healings and miracles that first year than I had in my entire life. Yet the greatest manifestation of His presence came through prophetic gifts. It was as if the veil had been lifted and people were able to see into the spiritual realm for the first time. Altar calls were no longer random pleas for people to come forward; we had specific calls for specific sins that God revealed. The physical needs in the body of Christ were called out through words of knowledge, and God met those needs. The atmosphere was charged with God's presence, and many within our congregation were able to see with a spirit of revelation (Eph. 1:17–18). We experienced miracles, healings, deliverances, salvations, and sanctifications. People became aware of their spiritual gifts, and we realized as a church that we needed to discover how to facilitate the deployment of these gifts biblically and purposefully.

All of these changes created a challenge for me. I have been raised in the Church of the Nazarene, and that had been my only ministry context since I started preaching in 1983. While our denomination was birthed in revival fires and has an idea of the power of the Holy Spirit, we don't have many paradigms in our movement for operating in the supernatural gifts of God — at least in the United States. The Church of the Nazarene has emphasized sanctification (or the baptism of the Holy Spirit) in terms of purity from sin, but has not pursued the empowerment for life and service, particularly in terms of the gifts of the Spirit (*charismata*). As a result, by the end of 2007, I was desperately searching the Bible and asking a multitude of questions about how to steward a culture where the supernatural gifts could be manifested.

Foundational to this search was my passion to fervently preach the message of holiness. I was not about to neglect, soften, or water down the preaching the truth of God's Word.

In fact, we saw many more experience sanctification and a purified heart during the first year after returning from my sabbatical than we did during the first nine years of the existence of Crossroads. I would not compromise the Word or the message of purity, but I was not going to resist the supernatural move of the Holy Spirit that was coming in power, signs, and wonders. I sought God for balance; I was certain Word and Spirit, or purity and power, could and must function together.

God is faithful; and by His mercy and grace, He began to teach me that the message of holiness accompanied with power could and should be expressed in a supernatural manner. For the first time in my life, I saw a convergence of purity and power. I realized that both were not just possible; they were indispensable and interdependent, and we needed the Word and the Spirit. It was out of this time of personal growth that a discipleship curriculum was written called *Living in the Supernatural (LS)*.[2] This is a discipleship training experience that combines the Word and the Spirit, and it activates the gifts of the Spirit in believers. This course is briefly described in the appendix.

The Church of Jesus Christ must experience this fusion of purity and power. If we do not capture the potential of both aspects, we will continue to be fractured and impotent. God has led me to pour out my life to see the merging of these two aspects: Word and Spirit, doctrine and display, form and fire, character and *charismata*, purity and power. Much of the Holiness movement has been divided and separated for the last one hundred years. Churches have camped out on one side or the other of purity and power. As you continue to read, you will learn why a division occurred, and what happened to spawn that division. You will come to understand that Word and Spirit cannot, and should not, be separated the way they have. It is time, said Jack Hayford, to "commit ourselves to a supernatural ministry, disciplined by a crucified life."[3]

Chapter Two

Defining Word and Spirit

⸺☙⸺

I t's an old, familiar adage that goes like this: "You can't have your cake and eat it, too." Mothers used this line for years to convince kids that they had to make a choice. Years ago, I heard a leadership expert lecture about the tyranny of the "or." He was arguing that in many cases, we don't have to choose between two opposing extremes. Instead of the "or," he argued, we should consider the blessing of the "and." We can have both the Word *and* the Spirit; we really can! Worship can be inclusive of "Spirit and truth." We can experience encounters with the presence of the Spirit and instruction through thoughtful biblical exposition. We can hear God's voice, and we can receive direction from the written Word. I'm saying that we can have all of the Spirit, and we can have all of the Word, both together: the blessing of the "and."[4]

Over the last few decades, the subject of uniting Word and Spirit has been a growing concern for Christian leaders. In October of 1992, Paul Cain and R. T. Kendall, two leaders on the opposite side of the fence, met together in London, England, to discuss the fusion of Word and Spirit. Their conference was an ardent plea to join these two concepts: the union of the character of the Word and the anointing of the

Spirit. Writing in the introduction of the book published from the conference lectures, Colin Dye stated:

> Instinctively we are seeking to bring together into mainstream Christian experience the correct balance and harmony between the Word and the Spirit. It is biblically incorrect to speak about the two in separation ... this revival may prove to be the long awaited "Isaac"— the Church of power and purity.[5]

This type of revival in the Church is something that I long to see: a revival of the Word and the Spirit, especially within the Holiness movement. Some actually believe that this union will usher in a new Great Awakening.[6] While progress has been made toward this effort, we still have much work before us if we are to see Word and Spirit united.

In Matthew 22:29, Jesus said that the Sadducees were mistaken; literally they were being led astray. This reference actually means to be in a state of confusion, to cause one to stagger and wander about because they are so badly misled. The reason for this staggering state was twofold: these religious leaders did not know the Scriptures (the Word) or the power of God (the Spirit). Because each of us comes from different experiences and backgrounds, I don't want to assume that we have common definition for the terms *Word* and *Spirit*. As a result of these differences, allow me to give some definitions for our foundation.

The Word of God

It was Jesus who said these religious leaders did not know or understand the Scriptures. Other than the writings of Moses, the Sadducees did not adhere to the words of the prophets, and they put little credence in the words of Jesus.

Unlike the Bereans in Acts 17:11, who studied and searched the Scriptures daily, the Sadducees were being taken down the wrong road because of their ignorance of Scriptures. You can just imagine what these leaders were thinking when Jesus told them that they were mistaken. This statement stung deeply and most likely offended them because it underscored their ignorance, something they didn't think they were capable of because they were the Harvard graduates of their day. Despite all of our knowledge, we too are prone to be led astray if we're ignorant of the Bible.

The early Church was devoted to a body of doctrine (Acts 2:42), and Paul instructed young Timothy to hold tightly to the doctrine imparted to him (1 Tim. 4:16). Doctrine was essential to the early Church, and the thirty references to that word (doctrine) in the New Testament represent an active sense of instruction, speech, and exhortation that shaped the lives of so many early believers. To uphold sound doctrine, we must know the Word, the truth of the Scriptures, or we will be sorely misled and will find ourselves practicing things in the Church that have little to do with truth.

If you're familiar with history then you'll remember that in AD 64, Nero burned most of Rome and then blamed it on Christians. This event prompted a mass exodus in the church at Ephesus, and it opened the door to infiltrating heresies. Because of the growing threat, Paul emphatically charged Timothy with special instructions to remain loyal to the Word against false teachers. Paul's appeal was for doctrinal soundness, which actually began in 2 Timothy 1:13, challenged Timothy to thwart the advance of any heresy in Ephesus by preaching the Word. In 2 Timothy 4:1–5, Paul wrote,

> I charge *you* therefore before God and the Lord
> Jesus Christ, who will judge the living and
> the dead at His appearing and His kingdom:
> Preach the word! Be ready in season *and* out

of season. Convince, rebuke, exhort, with
all longsuffering and teaching. For the time
will come when they will not endure sound
doctrine, but according to their own desires,
because they have itching ears, they will heap
up for themselves teachers; and they will turn
their ears away from the truth, and be turned
aside to fables. But you be watchful in all
things, endure afflictions, do the work of an
evangelist, fulfill your ministry.

The threat of heresy was aroused in Ephesus because
sound doctrine was being replaced with fear, defections, and
desertions. The only sure combat against such a threat, then
and now, was and is the preaching of the Word. Be sober, Paul
said, endure hardships, do the work of an evangelist, fulfill
your ministry. How? The answer is loud and clear: preach
the Word.

Paul said that a time is coming when people will not
endure sound doctrine; rather, they will want to be pacified
with teaching that is pleasant to their ears. How sad is that?
If we cater to people's whims, then we will water down the
Word of God. Perhaps this is one of the reasons why Paul
said that difficult days are coming, times when people will be
"unholy" among many other things (2 Tim. 3:1–5). Paul actually stated that the days are coming when people will have a
"form" or "appearance" of godliness. In other words, people
will have no real character of holiness on the inside of their
hearts; they will be empty and hollow of any real spiritual
substance despite the external façade.

In the context of this unholy lifestyle that Paul alluded to,
he stated some very specific characteristics, such as the following: "Men will be lovers of self, lovers of money, boastful,
arrogant, revilers, disobedient to parents, ungrateful, unloving,
irreconcilable, malicious gossips, without self-control, brutal,

haters of good, treacherous, reckless, conceited, loves of pleasure rather than lovers of God" (2 Tim. 3:2–4). The remedy to correct those characteristics is to preach the Word—I charge you, said Paul, to preach the Word!

Paul continued, "All Scripture *is* given by inspiration of God, and *is* profitable for doctrine, for reproof, for correction, for instruction in righteousness, that the man of God may be complete, thoroughly equipped for every good work" (2 Tim. 3:16–17). How do we correct unholy lifestyles? How do we reproof believers who are conceited, or are gossips, or are arrogant? We do so by using the Word of God. The Scriptures, rightly applied, have the ability to train us in righteousness. The Bible is living and active; it's the two-edged sword that penetrates the intent of our hearts (Heb. 4:12). Preaching the Word always sets up encounters with God's presence. We must be a people of the Word; we must hold to the Scriptures, we must preach sound doctrine.

I'm very concerned these days when I hear sermons that rarely make any reference to the Bible. Preachers might allude to a passage here or there, but the truth of God's Word seems trumped by stories, quotes, and recent book reviews. Each of these have their place in teaching and communicating, so by all means be creative and use them when preaching. However, nothing can equip believers like the Word of God, nothing possesses the inspiration to correct and train us, and nothing will prepare us for every good work like the Scriptures. The mystery of the Word of God is that it speaks to all people in every situation; therefore, we must make the Bible the main source from which we teach. Don't ever be ashamed to say to a congregation, "Please open your Bibles (or iPads these days)." Let the truth of God's Word challenge, convict, teach, train, and equip people.

God told young Samuel that He was about to release the Word upon him, and when that would happen, God said both ears of everyone would "tingle" (1 Sam. 3:11). By contrast,

Paul said a time will come when people will want their ears to "tickle" (2 Tim. 4:3). In other words, people will desire to hear pleasant lessons that make them feel good but don't challenge their present realities. If pastors, teachers, and leaders fall prey to catering to the whims of people, we'll simply tickle people's ears with messages containing no power of truth. I'm challenged most when I hear biblical truth taught because the Word lingers long in my heart. The Bible, uncompromisingly taught, will plow the fallow ground of people's hearts and implant the seed that will sprout a harvest of righteousness.

On the Day of Pentecost, Peter preached the Word to the multitudes, and at the end of his short sermon, the Bible says the hearts of the people were "pierced" (Acts 2:37). This word *pierced* is only found here in the New Testament, and it is similar to ears tingling as God told Samuel. To be pierced by the Word also indicates that people's hearts were sharply stung to the point that action was required. At the end of Peter's message, three thousand people were moved to respond. Peter's method was fairly simple, he just preached the Word.

Recently, I was preparing a message to deliver on Easter Sunday. I was intrigued by the passage in John that describes the disciples in a room with the doors shut, and they were in that very condition largely because of fear (20:19). The disciples were locked in a room and immobilized by fear on the very day that Jesus rose from the dead; they were bound by the stronghold of fear, and they were unable to believe the truth that Jesus was alive. Mary had even told them a few hours earlier that she saw Jesus alive, but they did not believe her. Then I discovered the reason: earlier Peter and John looked into an empty tomb and the Bible says they believed, yet they didn't know the Scriptures (20:8–9). Their faith was not tethered to the Word; they were ignorant to the Scriptures. Like Peter and John, we will always be subject to strongholds and false reasoning when we don't know the Scriptures.

Think about it; all faith must be attached to the Bible, or we will be carried away by every wind of doctrine. So let me ask you: how well do you know the Scriptures? Is your faith anchored to the Bible, or are you ignorant of what it actually says? As I travel and preach in churches, a deep concern grows in my spirit that people truly don't know the Word of God. We've settled for simple devotional books that skim the surface of Scriptures. We simply must *know* the Scriptures. My challenge to you is read your Bibles, and then read them again and again. Stay in a certain passage for a while, or "take out real-estate," as I like to say, until you know the context, the meaning, live it out, and become saturated in and through it. These days we have easy access to enough resources to help us all become better students of the Bible. So when I refer to the Word, I'm talking about an adherence to the Bible and the lifestyle that accompanies sound doctrine. I might talk about purity, character, or holiness, but it's all referring to the same idea that we must be a people of the Word, or else we will be devastatingly misled, just like the misguided Sadducees that Jesus rebuked.

The Spirit of God

The other part of Jesus' rebuke toward the Sadducees was that they failed to understand the "power of God." The Greek word for "power" is *dunamis,* which is a miraculous power or the capacity to perform an extraordinary, supernatural ability. *Dunamis* is a power orchestrated not by human talents, abilities, or efforts; rather, it is a power generated by the Holy Spirit. Unlike contemporary believers, first-century believers understood—and assumed—the Spirit to be manifested in power.[7] So when we talk about the Spirit, we are referring to the supernatural power that can only be generated by the Spirit; without the Holy Spirit, believers would have no power over sin, the enemy, or the flesh. Additionally,

35

power for miracles and gifts are generated by the work of the Spirit; therefore, to perform the deeds of Jesus we must be possessed by the same Spirit as Jesus was.

In the context of Matthew 22:29, the Sadducees were ignorant to the power of God because they failed to believe that God would raise the dead. They also did not believe in the power of God manifested in Jesus' earthly ministry, and this disbelief caused many needless debates with Jesus. Jesus' three-year ministry was marked by supernatural power, and those who rejected Jesus in turn rejected the Spirit that generated this power through Him. The Bible says that Jesus was led by the Spirit into the wilderness, but He emerged out of the wilderness in the "power of the Spirit" (Luke 4:14). His inaugural message in the synagogue at Nazareth (on the Sabbath) began with Him stating that the Spirit was upon Him to preach, heal, liberate, and recover sight (Luke 4:18). The Spirit's supernatural power was upon Jesus as He "went about all Galilee, teaching in their synagogues, preaching the gospel of the kingdom, and healing all kinds of sickness and all kinds of disease among the people" (Matt. 4:23).

Some scholars refer to this power as being "charismatic" in the sense that the Holy Spirit operated *through* Jesus; it was not conjured up or resident in Him, simply because He was God. This power was given to Him because the Spirit of God rested upon Him. Using the term "charismatic" does not mean a movement, church, or denomination. The word is derived from a Greek word, *charis,* which means grace. To function charismatically simply means living in the power of God's grace, and this generally includes functioning in the *charismata,* the plural for spiritual gifts, that is, God's graces, favors, or bestowments.[8] Jesus' entire ministry was marked by the work of the Spirit manifesting through Him. He preached the Word, but He also functioned in supernatural power.

36

The blessing of this power (*dunamis*) is that it is made available to all of us when we are baptized with the Holy Spirit. Prior to Pentecost, Jesus told His disciples, "I send the Promise of My Father upon you; but tarry in the city of Jerusalem until you are endued with power from on high" (Luke 24:49). Jesus told them to "stay"; this was an essential command. They were to remain, tarry, and go absolutely nowhere until they were endued with this power. In other words, they were not rightly clothed for ministry until they were empowered with the Holy Spirit. The same condition is true for us today. Not one of us is ready for ministry until we are clothed in the power of the Holy Spirit.

This power that the early church was clothed in made them impervious to forces that worked against them, and it grew this fledging church well beyond the city walls of Jerusalem. Professor of History at Yale University, Ramsay MacMullen, once wrote that these early believers possessed a power, which transformed people amidst a Roman pantheon; the undeniable power of the New Testament Church led secular, paganized people to "confess the one and only God of the Christians."[9] His book documents unparalleled stories of Christians demonstrating a power that was supreme to the false gods that people worshipped in Rome, during the first few centuries. Please note this discovery of the preeminence of power in the first centuries of the Church was not the conclusion of a charismatic Christian historian trying to prove a point but that of a secular historian from Yale.[10]

Paul's experience in Ephesus was a witness to this power, also. The city of Ephesus was a major city for trade in western Asia Minor during the first century. It was also marked by the pagan worship of the Roman goddess Diana. The people of Ephesus were not strangers to seeing "power" through their cultic practices, so Paul's messages alone were not enough to capture these people during his first few months of preaching (Acts 19:8–9). Much like what Moses encountered in the courts of Pharaoh, preaching alone sometimes will not convince people, but when Paul began to experience extraordinary miracles, Jews and Greeks dwelling in Ephesus began to turn to God. They fell before the power of God—a superior power—confessing and turning from their idolatrous deeds (Acts 19:18–19).

The same experience was witnessed in Corinth. Paul realized that superb rhetorical abilities could not compel people toward the gospel, so he said "my speech and my preaching were not with persuasive words of human wisdom, but in demonstration of the Spirit and of power" (1 Cor. 2:4). Paul did not want these people to place their faith in man's wisdom, but in the power of God. So the Word of God was put into action, and the Corinthian believers witnessed a superior power.

The world seems to recognize the authentic power of God; I just hope that the Church will again be able to. Years ago, A. W. Tozer explained that most churches could continue the ministries of their church in the absence of the Spirit for months, and yet many churches would not even notice the difference. He wrote:

> The essence of true Christianity is spontaneity—the sovereign movings of the Holy Spirit upon and in the free spirit of redeemed people. This has through the years of human history been the hallmark of spiritual excellency, the evidence of reality in a world of unreality. When Christianity loses its sovereign character and becomes mere form, this spontaneity is lost also, and in its place come precedent, propriety, system ... the belief that spirituality can be organized. Then is introduced into it those ideas which never belong there—numbers, statistics, the law of

averages and other such natural and human things. And creeping death always follows.[11]

That last sentence shakes me to my inner core, "creeping death always follows." Any church that adheres to programs, formats, and agendas more than they adhere to the Holy Spirit will eventually stagnate and die. Paul said, "Do not quench the Spirit" (1 Thess. 5:19). To "quench" the Spirit means to snuff out or suffocate a fire. Deprive a fire of oxygen for very long and see what happens; it will eventually die. I agree with Jim Cymbala, "Our attempt at ministry will be an absolute exercise in futility if we are not expecting and experiencing divine help through the power of the Holy Spirit."[12] Power is not some sort of add-on to the gospel; power is the essence of the gospel rightly taught (Rom. 1:16). We should always expect the Spirit of God to move when we've preached the Word.

I have come across believers who love the Word of God, yet they aren't so keen about the Spirit and His "sovereign movings," to use Tozer's words. During a conference recently, I observed a speaker who loved and communicated Bible truths well; yet amid the invitation given by another speaker, they sat seemingly unmoved as people were being touched by a fresh outpouring of God's Holy Spirit. Later conversations with this person revealed that they felt more comfortable with Bible truth than the moving of the Spirit (if that's even possible). We are to be ministers of the New Covenant, Paul said, not of the letter but of the Spirit as it is the Spirit that gives life (2 Cor. 3:6). The Bible, rightly taught, should lead us into an encounter with the presence of God. The Word should link us to the Spirit; truly they should be inseparable.

When the Spirit of God comes, He comes in power. Jesus said in Acts 1:8 that we will receive power when the Spirit is poured out. This power, generated by the Holy Spirit, is equivalent to the power that Jesus functioned with; there is no difference. We didn't get a "lesser" or mutated Holy Spirit, we received the same Spirit that Jesus received. Without this power, we will not only fail to bear fruit and conquer the flesh, but we will fail to be the kind of witnesses for God that only comes when the power of the Holy Spirit is manifested through our lives. And most certainly, we will be unable to represent the kingdom of God with extraordinary abilities because "the kingdom of God is not in word but in power" (1 Cor. 4:20).

Therefore, we must adhere to the Word of God and operate in the power of God's Spirit; to be like Jesus, we will function in the Word and in the Spirit. Jesus' rebuke in Matthew 22:29, represents a warning to all present-day believers. We must understand and embrace the Scriptures (Word) as well as the power (Spirit) of God. Both are essential, and both must function in tandem through our lives and throughout our ministries. Otherwise, we will be easily led astray like the Sadducees.

A Costly Divorce

Jack Deere, former associate professor of Old Testament at Dallas Theological Seminary, talked about a costly divorce between the Word and the Spirit. Like all divorces, they are painful for the children and the parents. Usually one parent will get custody of the children while the other parent gets visitation rights. When the Word and the Spirit are separated, churches, like children of a divorce, live with one parent or the other. Some churches are living with the Word, and every now and then, the Spirit gets to visit. You will recognize these churches because the "children" talk about *hearing* a great word. They are cautious when the Spirit comes for a visit, and sometimes these churches are even a bit uncomfortable until the Spirit leaves. Worse still, there are those in these churches who don't even recognize the Spirit when He comes.

On the other hand, there are churches living with the Spirit. The "children" of these churches speak about *seeing* the Spirit doing great things in the services. These churches can be very active, even a bit unruly at times in their services, and every now and then the Word visits, but it doesn't receive the same respect as the Spirit. The presence of the Word is treated with less value than the activity of the Spirit. Sometimes the reaction of the children of the Spirit is less than positive when they encounter the Word. They sometimes feel that the Word has come to condemn them or stifle their freedom. Deere closed his analogy by writing:

> So the Church has become a divided family growing up with separate parents. One set of kids is proud of their education (in the Word), and the other set of kids is proud of their freedom (in the Spirit). Both think they're better than the other. The parents are broken-hearted because unlike most divorces, they didn't choose this divorce. Their kids did. And the Word and the Spirit have had to both honor and endure that choice.[13]

The Word and the Spirit belong together. The Church will be healthier and stronger when they function as a married couple. We will never be Christlike unless we operate in the fusion of Word and Spirit. When Luke wrote the book of Acts, he began his prologue by chronicling the activities of Jesus (the activity of the Spirit) and what He taught (dispensing the Word). We, as the children of God, must demand that the divorce between the Word and the Spirit ends. And then, we must be willing to do what is necessary to unite them once again.

Throughout this book, I will interchange the Word and the Spirit with purity and power because they represent the same idea. The Holiness movement has taught the Word of God in terms of purity—the message of sanctification. We've generally accepted that sanctification purifies the heart from the propensity of sin; yet we have been cautious, even skeptical, of talking about the power of the Spirit being manifested by spiritual gifts through a sanctified individual. So when I refer to the Word and the Spirit, I'm also alluding to purity and power—purity as holiness of heart and life (as seen in the Word) and power as referring to the activity of the Spirit through supernatural functions (as seen in the lifestyle of Jesus). Also, while I'm adamant about the Word and the Spirit being united, I will extend the boundary just a bit toward the Spirit or the expression of power because most people within the Holiness movement (non-Pentecostal churches) have been living with the Word (embracing purity), but they are usually cautious about the Spirit's visitations of power. Let's take a look back at church history and discover where the divorce of Word and Spirit began.

Chapter Three
A Glimpse of Early History

———∾∾∾———

Where We Went Wrong (Part One)

C hurch history is peppered with people who made tremendous contributions to Christianity. We are indebted to so
many who made costly sacrifices for the cause of Christ and
laid the foundation that we build upon today. One such person
is John Wesley. Growing up in the Church of the Nazarene,
I often heard his name among others who contributed to the
Holiness movement. Considering he has commonly been
understood to be the father of the Holiness movement, his
name should not be absent from our history and heritage. In
fact he is believed to be the spiritual father of more than thir-
ty-five denominations and movements beyond the Methodist
church, including Pentecostal, Nazarene, Holiness, Renewal,
and Charismatic groups.

Wesley was an ardent student of the Scriptures and a
strong advocate of doctrine and form, but he found himself
challenged by the peace and presence of God that rested upon
a group of German Moravians. Wesley observed a *power*
manifesting through these Moravians amidst a storm that
caused many to scream out in panic and fear. Hounded by
the reality of the presence of God that they possessed, Wesley

43

pressed into God with deep repentance. It was not long until he experienced the infamous Aldersgate encounter where his heart was "strangely warmed." Later, a second deeper work of grace (known as entire sanctification) occurred, an experience that seemed to weld Word and Spirit in his life.

After Wesley's Aldersgate experience, a Moravian-style love feast occurred, an explosive revival that we should pine for today. Wesley recounted:

> As we were continuing insistent in prayer, the power of God came mightily upon us, insomuch that many cried out for exceeding joy, and many fell to the ground. As soon as we were recovered a little from that awe and amazement at the presence of his Majesty, we broke out with one voice, "we praise thee, oh God, we acknowledge thee to be the Lord."[14]

This account is just one of many where the power of God fell upon Wesley after his encounter with the Moravians. Wesley was never the same, and from that point on, his life and ministry personified the blend of preaching the Word and displaying supernatural displays of the Spirit's power.

It would be difficult to overestimate the influence that Wesley had in bringing renewal to England. Archbishop Davidson observed, in 1928, that Wesley practically changed the outlook and even the character of the English nation; in 1922, British Prime Minister Lloyd George said the Wesleyan movement was responsible for a complete revolution affected in the whole country of Wales, and it was impossible to explain nineteenth-century England without first explaining Wesley.[15] In fact, George went on to state that one cannot understand twentieth-century America if he or she does not understand Wesley.

Wesley had a clear understanding of holiness. His views of entire sanctification were spelled out in his *Plain Account of Christian Perfection,* and they brought to light what many writers before him had attempted to articulate. Of course, Wesley did more than simply preach the Word. Unlike many theologians of his era, he actually spent time "doing the stuff," and that included the display of miracles.[16]

It cannot be disputed that Wesley and the Methodists expected supernatural manifestations, signs, and wonders everywhere they went. Unlike much of the thinking that emerged out of the Reformation (namely that spiritual gifts were no longer necessary), Wesley believed in and practiced the spiritual gifts. When writing to the Methodists, explaining crucial principles, Wesley wrote the following concerning the supernatural:

> I do not know that God hath anyway pre-
> cluded himself from thus exerting his sov-
> ereign power, from working miracles in any
> kind or degree, in any age, to the end of the
> world. I do not recollect any Scripture wherein
> we are taught, that miracles were to be con-
> fined within the limits either of the apostolic
> or the Cyprianic age; or of any period of time,
> longer or shorter, even till the restitution of
> all things.[17]

The extraordinary gifts of the Spirit were such a contrast to the popular thinking and practice of the Church in Wesley's day. He believed God was capable of doing the supernatural through Christians, yet hindrances arose not merely from cessationism but from the general coldness and deadness of the fallen state of the Church. Wesley penned a sermon, stating that the root cause for the loss of the extraordinary gifts of the Holy Spirit in the Christian Church was because Christians had turned to heathenism again and had only a dead form left.[18]

It would be easy to read through that statement and continue to plow through this book, but we need to pause for a moment, perhaps much longer than a moment and deeply consider that statement. Has anything really changed over the years? Before we return to history, let's take a moment to analyze the present condition of the Holiness movement that was so powerfully birthed into existence through Wesley.

The Present Demise of Word and Spirit

What can we say about the present-day Holiness movement? Have Christians turned heathen again as Wesley so boldly proclaimed? I remember an interesting lecture given while I was attending the Nazarene Theological Seminary in 1989, outlining the five stages that all denominations and movements progress through within a one-hundred year time frame after their birth. Let me briefly outline these stages in response to where the Holiness movement might find itself today.

The first stage is called the origination or the movement phase. This phase is usually identified by a small group of individuals who are overtaken by a vision and the life-changing power of God. There is great excitement, energy, and optimism to propagate the gospel while advancing their God-given cause. The second stage is called the expansion phase. During this phase, the small group evangelizes, reaches out, and attracts new adherents. Growth and expansion occurs, and the new converts are marked with the same enthusiasm as the original group. The mission is still clear, and new adherents are discipled around the goals, purposes, and doctrines of the founding group.

The third stage is called the organization phase. During this phase, the original group has expanded to the point that it requires a degree of structure to maintain and perpetuate onward growth of the movement. Organization includes items such as effective discipling methods, managing resources, building healthy infrastructures, and maintaining divine momentum. The most essential aspect during this phase is to reacquaint the constituents of the organization with the founding values, purpose, and mission of the movement, and to quicken the hearts of its adherents with the same fervor and passion for God that the founding forefathers possessed.

However, and this is the point that I remember so vividly, historically there has never been a denomination that has successfully accomplished that endeavor; in fact, every group has ventured into a fourth phase called institutionalization. At this point, the group or denomination has become so diversified that it loses its true values and sense of purpose. Worse still, it has become so large that it is almost self-absorbing. Generations have now been born into the movement, but they have little knowledge of the experiences of past generations by which the foundation of the denomination was built upon. This lack of personal knowledge or experience gives birth to confusion and false doctrines.

If correction does not take place during the fourth phase, the denomination enters a final stage which is called stagnation. This phase is one where the movement exists in name only, but in reality, it is spiritually benign; power and potential are all but lost. While there might be a few constituents who understand the original calling of the organization, on the whole, the original vision and purpose of the entire denomination has died. Generally at this point, there is a split, and factions will spin off to begin new movements that often reflect the original focus of the founding group. Ruthven comments on the decline of Pentecostalism with a similar paradigm of the following: "a man, a message, a mission, a movement, a monument, to a mausoleum."[19]

When the class was dismissed, I caught up with the professor who gave the lecture and asked him where he saw the Church of the Nazarene in regards to these five stages. That moment is etched in my mind because I remember the look on his face when I asked that question. He struggled to answer because of his assessment of the Nazarene denomination and her sister denominations. He said we were moving quickly toward institutionalization, and if something was not corrected soon, we would cease to exist as a movement. I remind you that conversation took place in 1989.

So what can we say about the Holiness movement today? Is it dead? Keith Drury believed so when he wrote, "We need to admit to each other that the Holiness movement is dead. We have never had a funeral. And we still have the body upstairs in bed. In fact, we still keep it dressed up and still even talk about the movement as if it were alive. But the Holiness movement—as a movement—is dead."[20] William M. Greathouse, General Superintendent emeritus of the Church of the Nazarene, once stated, "As any denomination or movement grows numerically and matures ecclesiastically, it faces two dangers: first, to dilute the original message and second, to divert the original mission." Has the movement, which began with such passion and conviction under the leading of Wesley, diluted its message and strayed from its mission? Are we a movement that is a dressed-up corpse?

In February 2006, Kevin Mannoia began a three-year project to study the concerns and decline of the Holiness movement. The project's name was the Wesleyan Holiness Study Project (WHSP), and it included representatives from a wide range of churches, including both Pentecostal and non-Pentecostal branches of the movement, as well as black and white denominations. The participating denominations were the Salvation Army, Church of the Nazarene, Free Methodist Church, Brethren in Christ, International Church of the Foursquare Gospel, International Pentecostal Holiness

Church, Church of God (Anderson, Indiana), Church of God in Christ, Shield of Faith, and the Christian & Missionary Alliance.[21]
The outcome of this study identified issues such as over-emphasis on church growth, legalism, spiritual decline, ineffective discipleship, and a powerlessness within believers. In the final analysis, suggestions were given for renewal that sounded like a return to a Wesleyan-style of ministry, including being filled with the Holy Spirit, walking in holiness, executing spiritual gifts, and compassionate care for the poor, marginalized, and needy; in short, a rebirth of Word and Spirit.

Their discoveries reveal a systemic problem that shows we are in trouble. The present condition of the Holiness movement is very different from its beginning roots. While many wonderful things could be reported, the overall outlook is not good. The writer of Hebrews warned us to pay close attention to what we have heard, or we will drift away (Heb. 2:1). Drifting occurs so slowly and gently that you don't realize that it is happening. Unless you are keeping your eyes and perspective locked onto a stationary landmark, you lose perspective of how far you have deviated from the course. If we compare ourselves to Jesus or even the New Testament Church, which should be our stationary landmarks, we are vastly off course. I agree with this study by Mannoia; we must have a remarriage of the Word and the Spirit.

The Historical Demise of Word and Spirit

So where did the divorce between the Word and the Spirit begin? There had to be a time when people started to separate the supernatural from the preaching of the Word. No doubt Jesus encountered criticisms with the display of miraculous powers, but the real contention was launched against signs and wonders through the formal teachings of cessationism.

Cessationism is the teaching that miracles, signs, and wonders ceased after all the apostles died, and it became normative within Christianity in the first three centuries of the Church age.[22] After Christianity was legalized by Constantine in 312, a vast number of pagans joined the Church, which only fueled antagonism toward the work of the Holy Spirit and increased a bias toward cessationism.[23]

Augustine (354–430) introduced his theological début with cessationist sentiments, and it is fair to say that for the next one thousand years, he was the most important figure in the formation of the theology of healing (and nonhealing).[24] Although he refuted his views concerning cessationism in his later work called *The Retractions,* his influence upon theologians who followed was set in stone. His early writings concerning cessationism, despite his retraction, were read extensively by Martin Luther, John Calvin, and other Reformers, and cessationism became a foundational tenet for all of them.[25]

Later in history came Gregory the Great (540–604), whose cessationist tenets transmuted the miraculous *charismata* into more ordinary expressions of church ministry. For example, prophecy became preaching or teaching, and the miracles of healing became metaphors for regeneration: the "blind" see the light of the Gospel, the "lame" walk the paths of righteousness, and the "dead" are raised to newness of life.[26] This exchange not only downplayed the actual miracle events in the Bible, but it diminished the authority of the Scriptures. The Bible started to become what we wanted it to mean rather than what it actually said.

The problem of cessationism during sixth century was joined by a new religion that was developed by Mohammed (570–632), and it thoroughly saturated North Africa and the European continent. Soon power and corruption, along with religious depravity, overtook the Church which had a detrimental effect upon signs, miracles, and the supernatural work of the Holy Spirit. Incidentally, the Muslim religion is one of the fastest growing religions in the world.

Cessationist tenets continued from Thomas Aquinas (1225–1274), who taught that miracles served to guarantee the divine source and truth of Christian doctrines, particularly the deity of Christ,[27] to Martin Luther (1483–1546), who argued that miracles were particularly suited to the apostolic age and were no longer necessary to support the authority of one who stands on the side of Scripture. Eddie Hyatt argues that Luther's remarks were taken out of context and arranged into a legal system resulting in the Lutheran and Reformed wings of the church harboring a distinct bias against the possibility of present day miracles.[28]

Cessationism was solidified during the Reformation, when John Calvin (1509–1562) "popularized the restriction of miracles to the accreditation of the apostles and specifically to their writings."[29] In other words, supernatural power is what identified the apostles, and because they are dead, therefore so are miracles. This thread of reasoning served as the seedbed for the Enlightenment Era (1650–1790), a time in which "the basis of religious authority underwent a profound shift: from the Protestant basis of biblical authority to the human authority of perception and reason."[30] In short, we tried thinking apart from God.

The effects of this shift radically hindered the display of the *charismata* (the supernatural gifts) as well as the superiority of the revelatory voice of the Scriptures. The age of reason pushed for natural science and "common sense" thinking. Therefore, God's voice, or spiritual revelation, was thought to be inferior to the human mind and one's ability to reason. This age of thought opened the door to the philosopher David Hume (1711–1776), who became the most influential voice contributing to the long-standing modern prejudice against miracles.[31] Though Hume's work seemed to generate little interest in his day, much of the intellectual community eventually embraced Hume's approach and accepted that miracles violate natural laws and, hence, are therefore impossible.

The same year Hume produced his chapter, "On Miracles" (1748), Conyers Middleton (1683–1750) offered a similar essay called *A Free Inquiry into the Miraculous Powers*. His essay argued against the value of miracles. He wrote:

1. That they [miracles] were all of such a nature, and performed in such a manner, as would necessarily inject a suspicion of fraud and delusion.
2. That the cures and beneficial effects of them were either false, or imaginary, or accidental.
3. That they tend to confirm the idlest of all errors and superstitions.
4. That the integrity of the witnesses is either highly questionable or their credulity at least is so gross, as to render them unworthy of any credit.
5. That they were not only vain and unnecessary, but generally speaking, so trifling also, as to excite nothing but contempt.[32]

While Middleton's cessationist views were aimed at the errors of Roman Catholicism, he evoked a response from John Wesley, who believed Middleton was attempting to overthrow the entire Christian message. Wesley responded to Middleton with a rather bold letter, asking how it was possible that someone like Middleton could be so wise to believe the Bible, yet it seemed he believed everything but the Bible.[33] Wesley argued fervently in favor of the supernatural, yet in spite of his efforts, we can begin to see how the groundwork for the demise of Word and Spirit took root. In the next chapter we will explore some contemporary threats that attacked the Word and the Spirit. First, however, I want to return to John Wesley and briefly outline the Methodist revival as we entered into the 1900s.

The Historical Rebirth of Word and Spirit

There's no doubt that Wesley and his band of Methodists spawned a movement amid a time of upheaval of the Word and the Spirit initiated by apologists, theologians, and philosophers before and during his time. The theological breech that was left by cessationists was slowly being mended by the outpouring of the Word and the Spirit in Wesley's crusades and the campaigns of his contemporaries, such as George Whitfield and Jonathan Edwards and his successors Charles Finney, D. L. Moody, John Fletcher, and Phoebe Palmer. The rebirth was not easy, yet Wesley's message of entire sanctification, coupled with his Arminian theology of free grace, seemed to attract many searching for a deeper work of God in their lives. Additionally, many encountered a supernatural power that accompanied Wesley's message of holiness simply because the supernatural permeated his entire thought and life.[34]

Wesley did not incite emotion or "exercises" (manifestations of the Spirit) in his meetings, but the outpouring of God's Holy Spirit continued in an unprecedented manner. Grappling to comprehend these manifestations, Wesley would often journal his encounters. He once wrote:

> We understood that many were offended at the cries of those on whom the power of God came; among whom was a physician who was much afraid there might be fraud or imposture in the case. Today one whom he had known many years was the first who broke out into cries and tears. He could hardly believe his own eyes. He went and stood close to her, and observed every symptom, till great drops of sweat ran down her face and all her bones shook. He knew not what to think, being clearly convinced it was not fraud nor yet any

53

natural disorder. But when both her soul and body were healed in a moment, he acknowledged the finger of God.[35]

Over time Wesley's critics labeled him and the Methodists as "enthusiasts." It was a derogatory term aimed at those who experienced various manifestations when the Holy Spirit fell upon people during Wesley's meetings.[36] Wesley persevered with no less fervor despite the mockery, but his critics believed him and his band of followers to be excessively zealous. Historian Henry Rack wrote:

> Enthusiasm was the bugbear of decent and ordinary Anglicans, and was a charge which in many ways included all the others, for it implied not only religious excess but also social subversion. Its basic theological meaning in the eighteenth century was a claim to extraordinary revelations or powers of the Holy Spirit; and, more vaguely and abusively, any kind of religious excitement.[37]

Much of the ridicule occurred because Wesley's opponents believed the supernatural activity of the Holy Spirit to be "out of date." Rack went on, "Most of Wesley's educated contemporaries accepted that many of the charismatic phenomena of apostolic Christianity (including instant conversion) were confined to the apostolic age. In later times, sober teaching, right belief, and gradual process of religious nurture and development sufficed. Anything beyond this was 'enthusiastic.' The same applied to miracles"[38] We see once again the subtle influence of cessationism; yet, Wesley did not embrace the thinking of his Reformed brothers.

Although Wesley attempted to play down the supernatural claims that were happening in many of his meetings, Steve

Beard wrote that the manifestations of the Spirit "included the seemingly routine of people weeping, violently shaking, crying out, losing consciousness, falling down, and occasionally becoming uncontrollably agitated during his meetings."[39] Despite Wesley's uncertainty about these manifestations, Rack noted, he plainly thought they confirmed the truth of his cause.[40] That point is made clear when Wesley recorded the following account:

> I was led, I know not how, to speak strongly and explicitly of Predestination, and then to pray "that if I speak not the truth, He would stay His hand, and work no more among us. If this is His truth, He would not delay to confirm it by signs following." Immediately the power of God fell on us: one, and another, and another sunk to the earth; you might see them dropping on all sides as thunderstruck. One cried out loud. I went and prayed over her, and she received joy in the Holy Ghost. A second falling into the same agony, we turned to her, and received for her also the promise of the Father.[41]

Without encouraging or disparaging the extraordinary, it appears that Wesley relied upon the supernatural manifestations in his meetings as a divine sign to the truth he preached; thus, he continued in preaching the Word and practicing the miraculous deeds by the Spirit.

Methodism spread largely through Spirit-filled laymen, who forged a movement in America during the nineteenth and twentieth centuries. This spiritual movement attracted other laymen such as Ethan O. Allen, who was healed in a Methodist prayer meeting conducted by laymen.[42] Still others were attracted to the outpouring of God's Spirit, and the stage was set for an increase of revivals, outdoor crusades, and camp meetings across America. The Holiness movement was well on its way to becoming the dominant force in the land, coupled with its message of holiness (purity) and the outward manifestations of God's Spirit (power) through various healings and supernatural miracles.

Other voices, besides Wesley's, became known for purity and power such as Phoebe Palmer who toured the United States in the 1800s, encouraging people to receive the "baptism of pure fire," which was believed to bring about a purity of heart and an empowerment for ministry.[43] Palmer's infamous "altar theology" became the impetus behind the healing ministry that influenced many who followed her, believing that God's Word should be taken with absolute faith.[44] One such individual was Charles Cullis, who was not only influenced by Palmer but began a healing ministry in the late 1800s. Cullis taught many about healing and influenced practically every Christian healer of the next generation; among those he introduced to the healing ministry were the South African evangelist Andrew Murray and William Boardman, who established healing ministries in England.[45]

Perhaps one of the most influential Americans converted during the ministry of Cullis was A. J. Gordon, founder of the Boston Missionary Training Institute (Gordon College). Second to Cullis was A. B. Simpson, who was converted through the ministry of Cullis. Simpson disparaged the use of medications and went on to become a spokesman and leader of the faith cure movement; he made important contributions to the theology of healing, being one of the first to point out the relationship between Christ's atoning act and physical healing.[46]

What began in London in the 1700s when Wesley's heart was "strangely warmed" to a second crisis work of entire sanctification, now began to flourish as a dominant force in the late 1800s and into the early 1900s around the world.

The Holiness movement brought with it purity and power: a message of sanctification coupled to healing, miraculous signs, and wonders. However that move of God did not come without a battle yet to be fought. There were contemporary threats to the message of the Word and the Spirit that need to be addressed.

Chapter Four

Contemporary Threats (1900s)

---ᘒᙀᘒ---

Where We Went Wrong (Part Two)

Author and speaker Frank Billman noted that in 1890, Methodism was the largest Protestant domination within the Holiness movement in America, but he went on to explain that between 1890 and 1990, forty-five thousand Methodist churches were closed.[47] That fact alone is incredibly troubling to me. To think, a dominant force in the Holiness movement, such as Methodism, would begin to erode as we came into the 1900s should grab us by the shirt collar. Billman explains the reasons for this erosion are because voices rose up in the Holiness movement against the Word of God and the power of the Spirit.

Early on in the 1900s, theological liberalism began to shape the thinking of prominent theologians, and it overtook most of the mainline seminaries. Laurence Wood wrote, "The erosion of the Wesleyan doctrinal heritage occurred almost overnight when the leadership of the Methodist Episcopal Church changed hands from those committed to its Wesleyan heritage to those who were open to the newer ideas associated with liberal theology."[48] Historian Kenneth Scott Latourette said that liberalism had many and able exponents; they differed among themselves, but in general "they had confidence in human reason."[49] Consequently, essential Bible doctrines, including the doctrine of sanctification, were questioned. It was reasoned that man's efforts alone could achieve a standard of Christian excellence.[50] Even the "Restrictive Rule" that was adopted in 1808 that preserved the traditional Wesleyan doctrine of Holiness in Methodism no longer carried any value amidst the diversity and freedom of theological expression.[51]

But there were more threats to come. The writings and teachings of James Buckley in *The Christian Advocate* downplayed and criticized the supernatural work of the Holy Spirit among early Methodists, causing many within the Holiness movement to be sympathetic toward cessationism.[52] Many Methodists who were part of the Holiness revival since the days of Wesley left Methodism because of Buckley's influence.[53]

Billman posed an interesting thought when he wrote, "What the history of American Christianity would have been like if Methodism had become a Pentecostal denomination in the 1890s can only be imagined."[54] I have often had that same thought concerning the Church of the Nazarene. What could have happened if fear hadn't paralyzed us and dissention hadn't polarized us in the early 1900s? Sadly to say, critical voices of opposition led many within the Holiness movement to think differently toward the supernatural power of the Holy Spirit—and the Word—thus setting us on the course we are presently on.

Criticism toward the supernatural was compounded by Princeton theologian Benjamin Warfield through his writings and teachings, especially those expressed in his book, *Counterfeit Miracles* (*CM*) in 1918. Warfield's *CM* was written primarily because of the upsurge of miracles and healing that were occurring in American Protestantism across various movements and denominations during the last three decades of the nineteenth century.

According to Warfield, "spiritual gifts were given by God, transferred from the earthly ministry of Christ, to be distinctively the authentication of the apostles. They were part of the credentials of the apostles as the authoritative agents of God in founding the Church."[55] Like Calvin, Warfield believed that since the only function of miracles was to accredit revelation and because no new revelation was forthcoming after the apostolic age, miracles therefore must cease.[56] Warfield actually taught and wrote in *CM* the following extreme: "The Lord had not performed a single miracle on earth since the death of the original twelve apostles and those directly associated with them."[57] Therefore, argued Warfield, supernatural activities were strictly limited to the accreditation of revelation recorded in Scripture; any continuing activation of spiritual gifts for the express purpose of edifying the body of Christ would simply not be expected, necessary, or even permissible in his mind.[58] Unfortunately, people have embraced that line of reasoning today.

Warfield's teachings attacked those who believed in healing by his disregard and disagreement with the message of entire sanctification, a doctrine, I might add, that was the seedbed for healing within the Holiness movement. Warfield asserted that "while we are no longer under the curse of sin, as Christians, we nonetheless remain sinners. The struggle against 'indwelling sin' is constant, and continues through life."[59] Therefore, according to Warfield's reasoning, if we struggle against sin, we will experience a lifelong struggle against sickness. You can see that his teachings not only denigrated miracles, but the message of entire sanctification was questioned as well.

As for those who witnessed miracles or practiced healings, Warfield instigated a suspicion in people's minds toward them. Following Middleton's attempts to discredit those who reported post-apostolic miracles, Warfield challenged the witnesses' mental state and even their credibility. He would often note how reports of miracles may be generated by "blinding excitement," "brutal persecution," or by being inflamed by enthusiasm; if healings or miracles did occur, Warfield would attribute them to the power of hysteria or suggestion rather than to the power of God.[60] Consequently, the Church became suspicious of the supernatural.

In Warfield's Protestant attempt to protect the Scriptures, he actually created suspicion and doubt concerning God's Word. His teachings opened the door to higher, critical thinking, thanks to the Enlightenment Era that influenced him. As the Bible was questioned, belief was placed in mankind's own ability to achieve an ideal society.[61] The elevation of the mind made theology a science, on the same plane as other so-called "hard sciences," such as chemistry, biology, and astronomy; Warfield even exalted the mind and common-sense reasoning to an equal status with biblical authority.[62] This reasoning permeated the thinking of many Bible students and laymen like poison, and the foundation of Word and Spirit was severely damaged.

The Rise of Pentecostalism

Against the backdrop of cessationism and liberal views, there was a new and enthusiastic movement that came to the forefront in the early twentieth century. They called themselves "Pentecostals" because they looked back to the day of Pentecost and the outpouring of the Holy Spirit in the upper room as their inspiration.[63] In spite of persecution and slander, this group emphasized signs and wonders; and because of the enthusiasm and passion of this movement, the ground was fertile for revivals to spring forth. One such revival was the Welsh Revival in 1904 in Wales, spurred on by a coal miner named Evan Roberts, who witnessed the benefits of having prayed for God's outpouring for eleven years. This revival was marked by a remarkable freedom in the Holy Spirit, including "prolonged singing, lay preaching, testimonies, united prayer, frequent interruptions of the services by worshipers, and a heavy reliance on the inspired guidance of the Holy Spirit."[64]

By 1905, as reports of the Welsh revival spread, shock waves from this revival had reached Los Angeles. Holiness and Pentecostal communities began to pray, expecting an outpouring of God's Holy Spirit to fall. These meetings were spurred on by the previous influence of Charles F. Parham, a man who was generally recognized as the formulator of Pentecostal doctrine.[65] Among those influenced in these gatherings was a stocky African American man named William J. Seymour. So ignited by the message of holiness, particularly the baptism of the Holy Spirit with the evidence of speaking in tongues, Seymour began to preach anywhere he could.

On April 6, 1906, the power and presence of God fell on Seymour and a small group of believers. What began with a few people, lasted for several days; and the crowds grew until the little house they were meeting in was simply too small. One eyewitness related the story this way:

> They shouted three days and nights. It was Easter season. The people came from everywhere. By the next morning there was no way of getting near the house. As people came in they would fall under God's power; and the whole city was stirred. They shouted until the foundation of the house gave way, but no one was hurt.[66]

Eventually the crowds moved to a larger facility: a horse stable on Azusa Street, and the event became known worldwide as the Azusa Street Revival. Historians, as well as Pentecostals, point to this revival as the birth of the Pentecostal movement in America.

However, the excitement of this new movement, especially the aspect of speaking in tongues, was not fully embraced by certain holiness groups. Contention began to swell and a division emerged, a division that had a devastating effect on the relationship between Word and Spirit in the Holiness movement. Stephen Seamands identified this division as a "great divorce," and it separated the non-Pentecostals from the Pentecostals with a hostility that has lasted to the present. Summarizing the early 1900s, he wrote:

> In the first two decades of the twentieth century a great divorce occurred among two groups of Evangelical Christians—Holiness and Pentecostal—the effects of which we are still suffering from today. In light of how much they had in common, the divorce between these two groups was entirely unnecessary... the deeper issue of the conflict revolved around the nature of the baptism of the Holy Spirit, a spiritual experience that both groups strongly believed in. Yet they could not agree as to the nature of that experience: Was the experience primarily about *purity* (cleansing from a heart divided between self and God) or about *power* (anointing for ministry and service)?[67]

This divorce was tragic, given the fact that these two groups had so much in common. The conflict centered on the baptism of the Holy Spirit, which was an experience both groups strongly believed. However, the point of disagreement was on the nature of the experience with the Holy Spirit—was the experience about purity or power? Holiness groups that strayed from Pentecostalism emphasized the purity aspect of the Spirit, while those in Pentecostalism emphasized the power. I guess we couldn't conceive that it could be both.

Leaders in the Holiness movement such as Phineas F. Bresee, founder of the Church of the Nazarene in 1908, spoke out against the growing Pentecostals. Bresee's view of the Azusa Street Revival and its manifestations were noted as having the effect of a "pebble thrown into the sea."[68] Others stated that Pentecostalism was satanic and the last vomit of Satan.[69] By 1919, the Church of the Nazarene dropped the word *Pentecostal* from its name in order to avoid association with those who spoke in tongues. The hardline anti-Pentecostal attitude of many holiness people was summarized in Alma White's 1912 book titled *Demons and Tongues,* "which attributed *glossolalia* (tongues) to demonic influence."[70]

The dividing line between Pentecostals (who emphasized the Spirit: power) and the holiness groups (who emphasized the Word, specifically purity) only seem to widen as the years progressed. This disunion was unfortunate given the influence that Pentecostalism had within Christendom. By 1908, just two years after the Azusa Street Revival, Pentecostalism had expanded into fifty countries. By 1909, Pentecostalism had spread into China, South Africa, Chile, Argentina, and Brazil. By 1914, this movement had spread rapidly and established its home in every American city.

As Pentecostalism increased, so did the division with the traditional holiness church. Each group became known for their distinctive emphasis or cardinal doctrine. Vinson Synan wrote, "The original Pentecostals held to a basic belief in sanctification as a second work of grace and counted themselves as part of the Holiness movement, but they simply added a third blessing called the baptism of the Holy Spirit evidenced by speaking in other tongues."[71] Non-Pentecostal holiness churches, including the Church of the Nazarene, maintained a two-works doctrine emphasizing entire sanctification as the second work, only with no outward manifestation (specifically speaking in tongues).

Denominations that were established in the early 1900s (besides the Church of the Nazarene) rejecting Pentecostalism and speaking in tongues included the Wesleyan Methodist Church, the Salvation Army, the Free Methodist Church, the Church of God (Anderson, Indiana), and the Pilgrim Holiness Church.[72] At the same time these denominations emerged, a group of holiness churches formed that accepted the Pentecostal message of tongues. These denominations included the Church of God (Cleveland, Tennessee), the Pentecostal Holiness Church, the Church of God in Christ, the United Holy Church, and the Pentecostal Free-Will Baptist Church; these organizations all became the first organized Pentecostal denominations in America.[73] The division in the hearts of God's people between the Word and the Spirit seemed unwavering. .

So beginning in the early 1900s until the present day, those who have emphasized charismatic gifts have felt misunderstood by those who don't believe they are necessary. And those who have little or no place for the supernatural gifts feel threatened by those who believe they are necessary. Therefore, misunderstanding has led to criticism, disunity, and a loss of objectivity within the body of Christ.[74] The Word and the Spirit have been divorced.

Present-Day Challenges

Here we are, just over one hundred years after the formation of so many holiness churches and denominations. What can be said about the historic beginnings of Wesley and his band of Methodists? Have the early theologians maligned Word and Spirit with their cessationist and liberal views? Did the teachings of Buckley and Warfield influence contemporary evangelical theologians and their systematic theologies beyond repair? What about the contention that was spawned during the Azusa Street Revival between the traditional Holiness movement and the Pentecostals? These are critical questions still facing us today that demand our response.

Perusing the last one hundred years, there have been bright spots in our history where churches, movements, and denominations have flourished. I believe that we have taken steps in recent years to help bridge the divide between purity and power, between Word and Spirit churches. The two groups that evolved out of Classical Pentecostalism, Charismatics, and Neo-Charismatics still emphasize the *charismata*—miracles, signs, and wonders—but they have altered their dogmatic views of tongues that created so much tension in the early 1900s. And non-Pentecostal holiness churches are experiencing a renewal, of all things, in the power of the Holy Spirit.

My recent experience with the cohort for my Doctorate of Ministry afforded me the opportunity to hear the hearts of several prominent leaders both within the Charismatic movement and among other movements. They are deeply concerned about the deviation of central truths in the Bible within their denominations and movements. Moreover, they have expressed the need for holiness to be taught within their camps, and it is becoming clear that they are looking and hoping to bridge the divide that began in the early 1900s.

However, my concern is with non-Pentecostal holiness churches, at least for the purposes of this book. I have participated in roundtable discussions concerning the subject of supernatural gifts; they are being discussed and explored as necessary aspects of the sanctified life. Cross-pollination is taking place, and I am gratefully applauding every breakthrough that we have witnessed happening so far, yet there is more. In the midst of my optimism, I sense there is still much fear and reticence on our side of the fence. Some are still resistant to associate with Pentecostals and Charismatics out of suspicion that somehow we're going to be led down a road of sensationalism.

Moreover, the elephant in the room whenever we talk about manifestations and the supernatural within our churches is always the subject of tongues. I've been approached by leaders in my tribe during conferences, and their questions inevitably express their fear, or misunderstanding, about tongues. Suffice to say if tongues, or any of the supernatural gifts, *purposely* cause dissention in the body of Christ, they are not gifts operating through mature believers or, worse, believers not functioning in the Spirit of God.

I've also been intrigued and amazed by our steady diet of Reformed thinking and theology when we recommend and support books and attend seminars within our denomination, yet we avoid any writers or speakers who might sound like a Charismatic. My friend Kevin Seymour told me about his experience with a group of Nazarene pastors who gathered to study the growth patterns in the ten largest churches from various denominations in the United States. Despite the fact that the Pentecostal movement is one of the fastest growing denominations in the United States, to his amazement, not one of the churches on the list was a Pentecostal or Charismatic church. Kevin asked what the reason was for this apparent absence. No clear response was given. My only assumption is that we are afraid to get close to that side.

I had a very difficult time finding resources for my dissertation written by non-Pentecostal holiness writers, specifically from the Church of the Nazarene, which even addressed the subject of blending the Word and the Spirit. Even raising the subject with some people about blending these two concepts, I was told that it "sounds a bit charismatic." Beyond that, there are people in our tribe who still react publically or through media to this subject matter (talk about the supernatural, Charismatics, Pentecostals, and Word and Spirit) in some very hurtful ways.

While I agree that we've made some headway in bridging the divide, there are still too many churches on the purity side of the equation that have dried up while churches on the power side of the equation have blown up. We must eliminate fear and suspicion of "those people" and link hearts and hands for a common cause. If we ever hope to see citywide transformation, it will not happen through one church or denomination. It will occur when pastors, leaders, and laypeople of every Bible-centered, Christ-centered church follow the prescription in 2 Chronicles 7:14 of humility, prayer, seeking God, and turning from evil ways. During the process, form must unite with fire; doctrine must merge with display; and the Word must fuse with the Spirit.

Chapter Five

Understanding the Value of Theology

—⟡⟡⟡—

You are probably thinking right about now that a chapter on the subject of theology sounds about as interesting as having a root canal! Please don't skip this chapter because if we have wrong theological perspectives, we will inevitably find ourselves destroying the foundation for the Word and the Spirit to remain united. I want to begin by defining what theology is and then talk about the necessity of a right theology.

Defining Theology

Let's establish a working definition of theology. If you read the average theology book, the classic definition of theology is faith seeking understanding or faith seeking reason. To be honest, this definition stirs alarm simply because investigating and interpreting Christian faith to gain an understanding is not really possible outside of divine revelation. Without divine revelation, we start to elevate the mind over the Spirit. Let me clearly state that I am not advocating ignorance; I am, however, advocating the need to remain submissive to the greatest teacher of all, the Holy Spirit.

The ability to understand biblical truths is not possible apart from divine revelation. The power of reasoning and the power of the mind must remain dependent upon the Holy Spirit for inspiration. Otherwise, we will find ourselves back in the Enlightenment Era. When we make a conscience effort to seek the Holy Spirit, He leads you and He leads me into all truth (John 16:13), and when that leading is experienced, great things can be accomplished.

Consider the Hebrew Wisdom Literature in such passages as Proverbs 2:1–6 and in narratives that describe Solomon as receiving divine revelation as the source of his wisdom in 1 Kings 3:9, 12. Claims about God, as well as what we believe to be true about God, can only be given through the Spirit's revelation. The word *revelation* actually means the removal of a veil and a disclosure of what has been hidden. Revelation can occur through manifestations, appearances, visions, or simply a download of knowledge and truth into our hearts.

My point is that faith seeking understanding can only be possible as long as the seeker of understanding remains submitted to the guidance and voice of the Holy Spirit. Then, and only then, is the veil removed from our minds, enabling us to learn the deep things of God. Paul addressed this issue in the midst of a Hellenistic culture that prided itself in "wisdom" and supreme oratory abilities. The wisdom God speaks, Paul said, is hidden from those who avoid the Spirit of God. When we rely on the Spirit, things are revealed to us, even the deep things of God. The end result is that we can function with the mind of Christ (1 Cor. 2:16).

H. Orton Wiley, a well-known Nazarene theologian, described revelation as "a direct communication from God to man of such knowledge as is beyond the power of his reason to attain."[75] Jesus asked the disciples who they believed He was; Peter responded, and his response revealed that he was not reasoning out of his own capabilities. Jesus stated that Peter was hearing and receiving insight from God (Matt.

16:17). All theology must be dependent upon the revelatory voice of God speaking to an individual in a variety of ways, yet that doesn't negate the tethering of theology to the Word of God. Our knowledge of God is revealed through His Spirit, and all revelation must be congruent with the Word of God. Even John Wesley was accused of enthusiasm because he was open to the revelatory direction of the Holy Spirit, even the Spirit's manifestations, yet he repeatedly asserted the Bible to be the final authority in all matters that hedged his teachings.[76]

The best definition of theology, then, is faith seeking *more* faith (Rom. 1:17). That pursuit is an expression of the gospel in action; it is living by faith, and out of faith comes understanding (Heb. 11:3). To know God is to *know* Him, to seek Him with all of our heart, mind, and soul. Of course, we will never fully explain Him because He exceeds our explanations. Any attempt to hypothesize about God outside the guidance of the Holy Spirit is superfluous. Only when we are immersed in Him and experience more of the Holy Spirit can we ever hope to formulate a theology about Him.

I recently asked Jon Ruthven what his definition of theology is, and his response to me was the same: "faith into more faith." Then he wrote these words to me in an email. "In order to 'control' the often terrifying 'Word,' we want to talk it to death; if we can describe it, we can control it. It's the demonic strategy to try to inoculate people with an intellectual understanding of God to avoid their 'getting' it by revelation." Satan wouldn't have a problem with someone exchanging hypotheses about God, but he certainly doesn't want that person to have an encounter with Him. We are no real threat to the enemy by merely possessing an intellectual knowledge about God. Ruthven commented to me, "This kind of 'knowledge,' after all, is shared by the devil, who 'knows' theology better than any human." We should, however, desire to have an encounter with God, from which we will never be the same. What transformed the apostle Paul into a threat to the devil was not sitting at the feet of Gamaliel being educated (Acts 22:3), but sitting before the Lord. Paul was chiefly schooled through revelation (Gal. 1:12).

That being said, I'm not suggesting that we should avoid writing out theological perspectives, or even that theology books are inherently wrong. Effective theology can lay the groundwork that prepares us for deeper experiences with God. My concern is that we will stop short of divine encounters because we've settled for intellectual explanations about God. Proper theology should woo us into His presence; it should beckon us into intimacy with Jesus, so that we may hear and learn the mysteries of the kingdom. We should find ourselves stimulated with a hunger to pursue God because we've been taught a proper theology.

Theology is also practical in that it prepares us to make an impact in the world around us. Theology can be like salt that loses it saltiness if it remains aloof and distant or gets lost in theory, hypothesis, and speculation. Indeed the Hebrew concept of wisdom in the Old Testament always combined theoretical knowledge with practical skill and application. When Bezalel was described in Exodus 31:3 as being "filled with the Spirit of God," the result was that he was endowed by God's Spirit with *hokhmah,* "wisdom" or "skill" to design and build the various parts of, and items that filled, the Tabernacle. James Dunn stated, "Theology is not to be seen as simply something we observe and describe, but rather as something we do."[77] Theology should wear jeans or work clothes; it might get its hands dirty ministering to the needs of people. Gordon Fee called this "task theology," by which he meant a theology that was enacted in the marketplace.[78]

Beyond its working capacity, theology must also be dynamic; it must grow and develop as revelation increases. Even Jesus delayed giving revelation to His disciples until a later date; implied in His statement is that He had more to tell them but not at that moment, inferring that they would gain deeper truths at a later date (John 16:12). Theology has to grow and develop if it is to make any sense, or any difference, to the growing needs of people and to people as they themselves grow. To tuck theology away in a filing cabinet, untouched or even unchallenged from time to time, is worth very little.[79] We often treat theology as truths set in stone that emerged out of the Reformation that we dare not tamper with. Could it be possible, though, that the reformation of truth is still occurring? Could it be possible that there is more to our theology that the Holy Spirit wants to teach us? Mark Pfeifer poses the question, "When did the Reformation end?" His response is humorous, but made the point,

> If you ask a Lutheran that question they will tell you when Luther died. Ask most Baptists and they will tell you when John Calvin died. Ask most Wesleyans and they will tell you when John Wesley died. Ask the Pentecostals and they will tell you when the revivals of Azusa Street ceased. Ask most Catholics and they will reply, "What Reformation"? In my estimation, the Reformation has not ended; we are still in the recovery process.[80]

I don't think we should place a bookend on theological truths. Theology must expand and develop as its recipients mature and continue to seek God. Theology can never be bigger than God. While there are certain truths that are foundational and unchanging, God, through His Spirit, is still revealing secrets of the kingdom to those who avail themselves to Him (Matt. 13:11; 1 Cor. 2:9–10).

Before moving on, it is evident that this discussion has some profound implications for any denomination or movement, specifically the Holiness movement that rose out of the Reformation period. Dogmatic views concerning the doctrines of salvation, sanctification, and spiritual gifts that emerged directly out of the Reformation might need to be reconsidered in the light of deeper revelation. The point is, while we are thankful for the Reformation, some doctrines have been tucked away in filing cabinets since that period that might need to be taken out and reexamined in the light of actual biblical emphasis and revelation of the Holy Spirit.

The Necessity of Theology

What is the necessity of theology? Do we really need it? William DeArteaga asked a very pertinent question, "What happens when the Spirit gives His gifts but there is no theology to *receive* the experience [emphasis his]?"[81] Let's examine what insight the Word gives concerning that question. In Acts 2:13, the Bible says some people within the crowd, on the day of Pentecost, *mocked* the disciples' upper-room encounter. Their ignorance, or shall we say their lack of theological basis, led them to fear, speculation, and derision; they spurned an authentic outpouring of God that was demonstrated through signs and wonders.

Michael L. Brown, who experienced his own share of mocking during the Brownsville Revival from 1996 to 2000, stated in his preface, "Revival by its very nature generates controversy, and I do not know of any significant revival in recorded church history that has escaped its share of criticism and misunderstanding."[82] What causes this kind of reaction to the outpouring of God's Holy Spirit? Brown went on to state that revival "presents a challenge to the religious status quo, meaning that it can be perceived as a threat to the historical foundations of the faith."[83] Essentially, where there is no theological base, present moves of God's Spirit are dismissed, rejected, and even ridiculed.

It is interesting to note two thousand years ago, on the Day of Pentecost, a controversy over the outpouring of God's Spirit led to constant persecution upon the Church. Almost two thousand years later, the Azusa Street Revival received much of the same reaction. If theology does not expand and adjust under the direction of the Holy Spirit, the Church will continue to shoot down and ridicule present moves of God that does not reflect the theological boundaries so familiar to us.

Theology must expand, just as we see in Acts 15:28. The Jerusalem Council listened first to the Holy Spirit when they considered the theological and practical questions concerning the incorporation of Gentiles into the Messianic Jewish Church. This Council modeled for the Church of today our need to place priority on listening to God's Spirit, being willing to remain open to the revelatory leadership of the Holy Spirit, and then following His directives. Otherwise, as previously stated, history will continue to repeat itself with every fresh outpouring of God's Spirit. Theology certainly is not gullible, but theology that is Spirit-influenced will rightly discern and examine the practices of a movement without quenching the authentic outpouring of God's Spirit (1 Thess. 5:19–21).

So to answer the question, "Is theology necessary?" the answer is, yes, it is very essential! Please keep in mind that the "yes" carries with it the fact that theology is dynamic, is practical, and is shaped by the ongoing revelation of the Spirit at work in our lives.

The Theological Demise of Word and Spirit

All of this discussion about theology raises an interesting observation. If theology has been formulated incorrectly, it will be unable to discern just how and when the Spirit is moving or, even if such a move is necessary. Ruthven's recent book, *What's Wrong with Protestant Theology,* pinpointed this very issue. He asserted that the Reformation was overreactive in nature to the first fifteen hundred years of Christianity. Consequently, within the *protest,* errors were created that have altered the theological trajectory of Christianity for the last five hundred years.

The Reformers' message in reaction to the tyranny of Catholicism was ardent and clear: salvation is free! However, the message of salvation became centrally focused on heaven. The Holy Spirit's only role was to be active in preparing a person for heaven or the "born-again" experience, but very little was said about spiritual gifts, prophecies, or miracles until the time heaven is reached.[84] As a result of this emphasis, most of our Protestant theology has become a *theology of preparation.* Ruthven wrote:

> If we examine the preaching in a typical
> Protestant church we will discover a pattern
> of content that emphasizes our need for grace
> and our need to live out that grace by living an
> ethical life until we die and go to heaven, but
> imitating the New Testament apostles or Jesus
> in their exact way of presenting the kingdom
> of God is rarely mentioned, or, more often is
> discouraged.[85]

Salvation is much more than an insurance policy. The meaning of salvation in the New Testament carries the idea of healing, deliverance, restoration, and preservation. It implies the idea of empowerment for a cause. In the gospels, salvation not only included forgiveness of sins, but it primarily referred to Jesus healing and casting out demons; salvation for Jesus was inclusive of charismatic activity. Jesus sent His ministry teams out with the command to heal the sick, cast out demons, cleanse the lepers, raise the dead, and then tell people that the kingdom had come to them (Matt. 10:7–8; Luke 10:9). These activities were part of the salvation message.

If our immediate concern is "getting out of here" and going to heaven, we won't have much interest in developing a theology of charismatic ministry. I'm not saying that heaven is not a promised reality for the redeemed, and I'm not suggesting that we shouldn't attempt to convert sinners so that they can experience that reality. However, Jesus' immediate emphasis was not as much about getting to heaven as it was in doing the work of heaven here on earth. He taught His disciples to pray "Thy kingdom come" (Luke 11:2). Yet many believers today have adopted a theology of preparation and lost sight of their mission of touching lives. Go and make disciples, Jesus said, and the Holy Spirit will empower us to accomplish that task. That mission is to be our primary focus, not trying to get out of here as soon as we can.

Moreover, Protestantism limits or has little use for the prophetic voice of God because we have the Bible. Ruthven went on, "Every time we read about God speaking to one of his biblical characters, we semiconsciously *translate* the event: since God cannot speak directly to me today, how I apply this idea to myself is to remember that I only hear from God by *reading the Scripture* [emphasis his]."[86] In other words, many don't actually expect to hear God's revelatory voice as they read His Word. This thought process is an outright denial of the New Covenant Spirit promised by Jesus: the Spirit who fills and speaks to our hearts, and all generations to come (Isa. 59:21; cited in Acts 2:38–39).

This Protestant theological filter distorts how we interpret the Bible, too. We will extract portions of a text to support certain doctrines and in the process lose sight of what a passage is actually attempting to say within the context. Beyond that, miracles that Jesus performed and instructed His disciples to employ are turned into metaphors to support a Protestant gospel of salvation. We preach spiritual messages about the blind seeing spiritually, or the deaf hearing the gospel, or the lame walking the path of righteousness. While people may become born again, and I certainly celebrate that, the end result minimizes the primary emphasis of a particular passage challenging us to duplicate Jesus' ministry by actually doing what He did.

A central theme to the theology in the Holiness movement is the doctrine of sanctification. However, the emphasis of sanctification over the years, due to Protestant theology, has been on sin-avoidance and living an ethical life in preparation for heaven. While this aspect is part of the doctrine of sanctification, there has been a de-emphasis on the supernatural power of the Holy Spirit and the ability to flow in the *charismata* as a result of being sanctified. If we have the same Spirit who anointed Jesus and gave Him power for ministry, the *same* power will enable us for service.[87] "We cannot talk, at least in biblical terms," asserted Ruthven, "about being 'Spirit-filled' if there is no corresponding outworking of Jesus' charismatic ministry in our lives."[88] A sanctified people, filled with the Holy Spirit, will function as a charismatic community; this is grace coming to expression in Word and deed.[89]

Sanctification is a provision and blessing of grace, but it involves more than being cleansed from sin or set apart from something. Sanctification involves being set apart for God's mission, too; it doesn't mean just being saved *from* something, but *for* something.[90] Jesus sanctified His disciples for God's use; in being consecrated, they were able to *do* the truth, not merely remain holy.[91] Protestantism has robbed the Holiness movement of teaching the priestly function of fully sanctified individuals (1 Pet. 2:9), who when sanctified, are consecrated and empowered for the purpose of fulfilling a biblical role of speaking to God's people a prophetic voice of hope, healing, and deliverance. Sanctification implies a relationship with God where believers are "led" by the Spirit, actually fulfilling the holy functions of the priesthood with behavior that rightly reflects the power of the Holy Spirit.[92] Sin avoidance is only one half of being entirely sanctified, but being empowered with *charismata* to actually *do* the work of God, is the other half that has been overlooked by a theology of preparation. As stated before, the traditional definition of theology is faith seeking understanding. This view has warped much of the academics in the last few centuries because it builds a theological education upon the fruit from the wrong tree—the tree of knowledge rather than the tree of life. We were never made to eat from that particular tree. Implicit in the tree of knowledge is the power of our own reasoning over and above divine revelation, and even an arrogance about what we know intellectually (1 Cor. 8:1).

Most of our Christian education represents the traditional seminary approach to developing clergy (leaders) with an emphasis upon the acquisition of information rather than acquiring effective spiritual and ministry giftings. We assign rank and value to students, using such terms as grades, degrees, good or bad student, pass or failing, and so forth.[93] When they progress through this system and graduate, we assume that they should be prepared for ministry. We think that somehow because of their education, they will be effective in evangelism, prayer, demonstration of power, laying hands on the sick, or even a devotion to the presence of the Holy Spirit.

Yet, none of these charismatic activities are factored into the overall theological training process. Instead, the defining ranking is based wholly on what the graduate has intellectually grasped and verbalized during their Christian education. He or she is praised on academic excellence rather than the anointing and spiritual effectiveness that Jesus emphasized when He deployed His "students." The mind is elevated, as in the Enlightenment Era, to a superior status which precludes flowing in charismatic power. Let's be honest, we would be hard-pressed to identify very many seminaries willing to award a degree to a student based on how many people they raised from the dead. Certainly other factors need to be considered when handing out degrees other than charismatic activities.

The tragedy is, however, we have graduated many students through our holiness schools who can articulate intellectual insights, but they know little about deploying spiritual gifts; they have little understanding on how to operate in miraculous activities. And worse, these kinds of activities are often spurned in the "educated" mind and thought to be of lesser value to the ministry of the Church despite the fact that Jesus said that we were to duplicate and exceed His works.

Christian education in North America has been shaped by the English culture and the Enlightenment. The central goal of "higher education" has been the crafting of "learned gentlemen" whose academic credentials would assure status and power in the community. The Association of Theological Schools (ATS) soon adopted its criteria for awarding Bible degrees, not by a standard of ministry effectiveness but rather by a standard of scholarship.[94] And so, we have continued to feed food to students in colleges and seminaries from the wrong tree: the tree of the knowledge of good and evil rather than the tree of life.

At this point, you can begin to grasp why there was such a reaction to the outpouring of the Spirit at Pentecost, Azusa Street, the Toronto Blessing, the Brownsville Revival, or any other significant outpouring of the Holy Spirit throughout history. I'm not suggesting that every manifestation that surrounded some of these revivals was Spirit-led, either. I'm saying that theology always affects our interpretation of a particular event—especially a theology that believes the emphasis of the gospel is only concerned with preparation for eternity. Indeed, if we believe theological education is more about academic excellence than replicating the activities of Jesus, we will always react negatively to supernatural outpourings of God's Spirit. Our minds won't allow it. I want to suggest that we build a theology on what the Bible actually says. When we do that correctly, it will be a theology of the Word and the Spirit. So let's examine a theology based upon a biblical emphasis.

Chapter Six
Building a Theology of Word and Spirit

—⟡⟡⟡—

I f we hope to establish a theology that is inclusive of this fusion of Word and Spirit, we need to formulate theology correctly. The challenge is to develop a working theology that accurately reflects a biblical emphasis. Most people would argue that theology *is* built on the Word; however, I would propose that much of our theology has been formulated by traditional Protestant views. As Ruthven pointed out, "For all the emphasis that Protestants place upon Scripture as their ultimate doctrinal authority, they tended to use the Bible as a source for proof text rather than allowing it to speak with its own voice and emphasis."[95]

Too much of theology was written after deciding the message of Christianity, and that is an abuse of the authority of the Bible. The real issue when formulating a biblical theology is to discover what the Bible is trying to emphasize. Theologians rarely have asked what the Bible was attempting to emphasize; rather, they picked portions out to supplement doctrines. "Even the twentieth century Biblical Theology Movement," wrote Ruthven, "which aimed to let the Bible speak with its own voice, was influenced by pre-conceived themes from traditional theology rather than by the emphases of Scripture."[96] Doctrines should never override the central emphasis of God's Word, regardless of how important we believe they are.

What does the Bible say in its own voice? What is the Bible trying to emphasize? Certainly it advocates that there is a vast difference between *knowing* God (intimately) and knowing information *about* Him (academically). The Bible indicates that there were those who knew God's works, but they didn't know His ways (Heb. 3:8–10). I would argue that too many people, even in our churches today, know about His works. They have an academic knowledge and can describe things that He has done. Yet there are others who know God's ways; they know His heart because they have walked in intimacy with God. By exposing their lives to Him, they have drawn closer to God, and God in turn has drawn closer to them.

That kind of experience can and will shape theology because we realize that God is intimate and that we can walk with Him and commune with Him. God is closer to us than mere acts that He performs. Because we have been given the prophetic Spirit promised to us and bestowed upon us in the New Covenant, we can live in union with Him moment by moment. I'm the house of God! He dwells in me! Theology, then, should be shaped by that fact. Theology is much more than preparation for heaven. It becomes more than merely getting people saved so they are ready for death; rather theology becomes more about helping people *live* life.

Let's take it a step farther: what was the emphasis of Jesus' ministry? I ask this question because I believe the Old Testament points to Jesus Christ, while the New Testament is established on Him. Therefore, theology must be Christocentric. Moreover, the Holiness movement has always pointed to "Christlikeness" as the pinnacle of the holy life. So if we can establish what Jesus was attempting to *emphasize* in the gospels, then we should have a pattern to follow.

The entire rabbinical system of the first century was built on intimacy and emulation; a pupil was to be like their teacher, said historian Ray Vander Laan.[97] He went on to state, "Following Jesus isn't simply a matter of turning our hearts and souls to Him; it means taking the yoke of His teaching and living it out day after day."[98] If we claim to be followers of Jesus, then we must be committed to becoming exactly like Him in words and deeds. Simply, the goal of my life is to be more Christlike. Truly all theology should point to Christ and His lifestyle.

So, what did Jesus emphasize? To gain an overall understanding of Jesus' lifestyle, four essential questions need to be asked:

1. What is it that the New Testament says that Jesus came to do?
2. What did He actually spend His time doing?
3. What did Jesus tell His disciples to do?
4. What is it that they actually spent their time doing?[99]

The Bible summarizes the first two questions with a plethora of Scriptures by demonstrating Jesus in direct opposition to the devil by employing miracles, healings, and exorcisms.[100] Certainly Jesus did other things besides these kinds of activities, but if New Testament discipleship depends upon replicating the life of the exemplar, then miracles and the supernatural represent a significant part of our call to imitate Christ. We cannot sidestep the charismatic activity of the Bible and claim to have a theology that is biblically centered— at least a theology that replicates Jesus.

Jesus came to seek and save the lost, and He spent His time manifesting supernatural deeds to bring people into an encounter with the kingdom of God. His time was also spent mentoring His twelve disciples to duplicate His ministry, and much of that mentoring involved miraculous works. In fact, if we note the space devoted to miracles in the public ministry of Jesus that is recorded in the gospels, the percentages are very revealing: 44 percent of Matthew, 65 percent of Mark, 29 percent of Luke, and 30 percent of John.[101] Being like Jesus, at least in response to these first two questions, involves charismatic activity in our lives.

The last two questions are answered in Jesus' commissioning accounts to His disciples and specifically demonstrated in the book of Acts. It is important to note that 49.7 percent of the book of Acts is comprised of charismatic expression: miracles and prophecies.[102] These percentages should tell us that Jesus not only demonstrated charismatic power in His ministry, but He commissioned each of His followers to replicate His lifestyle. And in fact, they did!

There is no indication in the Bible that these kinds of activities ended after the apostles died or when the Scriptures were fully constructed. Any attempt on our part to suspend these kinds of activities is to view the Church as an institutional organization void of the dynamic, charismatic character of the primitive Christian community.[103] The American church is in desperate need of something besides institutional Christians who have a form of godliness but lack real power. Therefore, the biblical emphasis for any true follower of Jesus is that they will manifest charismatic power: healing, prophecies, exorcisms, and so forth. Truly, the "gifts (*charismata*) and calling of God are irrevocable" (Rom. 11:29).

I realize that theology is more complex and inclusive of other emphasis than what we've examined so far. To be fair, we could discuss other issues such as suffering, communion with God, the kingdom of heaven, or sin and redemption. However, the amount of time given by Jesus on charismatic works cannot be discredited or overlooked. Therefore, if we are to formulate a biblical theology, then scriptural emphasis demands that we include charismatic functions. I would label this aspect of theology as *power*: power of the Spirit that equips, anoints, and enables Christians to operate in super-natural ways, displaying the supernatural gifts.

However, there is another biblical emphasis that is imperative to include in theology and I would label it as *purity*. If we hope to express the *charismata* with any longevity, then it is essential to execute charismatic activity through a sanctified vessel. The Bible is replete with the need for purity (sanctification or holiness) of heart for all believers; otherwise, supernatural power will not be sustainable.

Looking into the Scriptures, the apostle Peter had something to say about purity after the Holy Spirit was poured out upon the Gentiles. His visit to these "outsiders" proved that *all* parties involved experienced the same result, namely a purified heart *and* the baptism of the Holy Spirit. Peter said, "So God, who knows the heart, acknowledged them by giving them the Holy Spirit just as He did to us, and made no distinction between us and them, purifying their hearts by faith" (Acts 15:8–9). Peter was referring to the outpouring at Pentecost when he said, God gave the Holy Spirit to them "just as He did to us." Prior to Pentecost, the disciples were unable to fulfill the commission that Jesus assigned; they needed something *more*. Most certainly they needed power (Acts 1:8), but Peter's report identified the fact that he, and the Gentiles, had their hearts purified in conjunction with receiving power.

King David must have understood the necessity of having a purified heart. He described what needed to take place in our lives when we come and dwell in the presence of God. "Who may ascend into the hill of the Lord? Or who may stand in His holy place? He who has clean hands and a pure heart" (Ps. 24:3–4). David possessed revelation that having our sins cleansed was only part of the requirement of being in a right relationship with God; the full revelation also revealed the necessity of a purified heart, which only God could do.

James exhorted Jewish believers to purify their hearts (James 4:8). He actually called them "double-minded" prior to being purified. This term is only used by James, and it describes someone who vacillates or is divided in their loyalties. James stated that "a double-minded man (is) unstable in all his ways" (1:8). Note that last phrase "in all his ways," meaning that all of life is affected by the duplicity of a heart that has not been purified. James identified the instability in these Christians, such as hearing the word but not doing it (1:22), believers showing partiality toward the affluent (2:4), claiming to have faith while demonstrating no works (2:14), a tongue that blesses God and curses people (3:9), and quarreling, arguing, and fighting among other believers (4:1); all of these activities warranted the necessity of their hearts being purified from the duplicity characterized in their lives.

This duplicity of the heart seemed to plague the Israelites, too, when they came out of Egypt. They constantly vacillated after their exodus, murmuring, complaining, and longing for the "good 'ole days" back in Egypt. The epitome of their duplicity was evident when the Scriptures says of them: "They made a calf in Horeb, and worshiped the molded image. Thus they changed their glory into the image of an ox that eats grass" (Ps. 106:19–20). The miracles and supernatural works of God were not enough to sustain their progress from Egypt. They had left Egypt, but Egypt hadn't left them. They needed the duplicity of their hearts purified. That's why God said, "Therefore circumcise the foreskin of your heart, and be stiff-necked no longer" (Deut. 10:16). The good news is that God loves us enough to get to the *heart* of the problem.

When John the Baptist prophesied about Jesus coming, he spoke of a baptism with the Holy Spirit and fire (Luke 3:16). Among other things, fire is a purifying agent. Malachi wrote, "He will sit as a refiner and a purifier of silver; He will purify the sons of Levi, and purge them as gold and silver, that they may offer to the Lord an offering in righteousness" (Mal.

3:3). Heaven's pattern still remains the same. God wants to purify for Himself a people to represent Him, so He sends His Spirit to purge our hearts, and then He anoints us to walk in righteousness. This baptism that John spoke about purifies our hearts from the chaff with fire and empowers our life with the Spirit to replicate Jesus.

The apostle Paul summarized ministry for a fledging Timothy by saying that the purpose of the commandment is love—but that love, Paul says, comes from a pure heart (1 Tim. 1:5). It is impossible to minister out of love without a pure heart, and without a pure heart the gifts will be skewed and poorly executed.

Purity, holiness, or sanctification is not a side issue, and it's not merely a "Nazarene" doctrine. Holiness is a biblical emphasis that is imperative to a biblical theology. I cannot overstate this, but without holiness we will not only fail to see the Lord (Heb. 12:14) but we will fail to see what is possible when power links with purity. Charismatic activities are disastrous without a theology of holiness. Unless we are crucified with Christ and set apart for sacred use, we will be too impressed by what we believe *we* can do.

In summarizing some of the mistakes made in the Charismatic Renewal over the last one hundred years, William DeArteaga stated, "The Charismatic Renewal, in its rightful rejection of the holiness patterns of legalism, inadvertently tossed out the Wesleyan quest for perfection and holiness of life as the goal of Christian life."[104] This was indeed a tragic mistake to make because a life of power must always be expressed through an agent of purity; otherwise, the duration and effectiveness of the supernatural will be short-lived. The example of Samson in Judges 13–16 demonstrates this very principle. DeArteaga went on, "The lack of the Wesleyan perfection component, plus the temptations of an exaggerated prosperity and tithing theology, was contributing agents to the exaggerations and scandals so destructive to the Charismatic Renewal."[105] We must fashion a biblical theology which embraces charismatic activities while still holding tightly to the experience of holiness so ardently emphasized in the Bible.

Stephen Seamands summarized the schism that took place in the early 1900s between the Holiness movement and the Pentecostals in a chapter called "The Great Divorce: How Power and Purity Got Separated".[106] He referenced a time in 1910, when entire sanctification was essentially denounced by a few people as a second definite work in Pentecostalism, emphasizing instead *only power* in the crisis of Spirit-baptism. This viewpoint sparked much controversy within the Pentecostal camps, but the outcome from the de-emphasis of sanctification was hurtful. Seamands wrote, "In addition then to its division with the Holiness movement over the relation of purity and power, Pentecostalism was now divided within itself over the issue (sanctification). The overall effect was to weaken the emphasis on purity within the movement, which arguably weakened the impact of the movement as a whole."[107]

Biblical theology, established on the emphasis of Scripture, will be inclusive of purity and power, in fact, it *must* be inclusive of the two. Yes, there are other components to a biblical theology, but these two, purity and power, comprise an overwhelming amount of biblical weight. Seamands concluded, "We must embrace a biblical and experiential joining of these concepts in our own lives so that we may realize all that God intends for His children in holiness, power, and life-changing influence upon our world."[108] This statement is not only well said, but it brings us to a crossroad. I pray that we will consider embracing a biblical theology that compels us toward God and to an experience with God that will produce people who are holy *and* activated—people who are sanctified, walking in holiness and empowered, executing the gifts of the Spirit.

Theological Implications

On September 26, 1965, the power of God's Holy Spirit fell on a group of Dutch Presbyterians and marked the beginning of the great awakening in Indonesia. Literally, tens of thousands of people came to faith, and nearly every single miracle recorded in the four gospels was duplicated through these Timorese people as they dispersed the gospel. While there were critics of the revival here in the West, the move of God captured the attention of G. T. Bustin. He was a district superintendent in the Pilgrim Holiness Church, a primitive holiness church that evolved from the early Wesleyan Holiness movement.

Bustin was a strong proponent and preacher of holiness, namely entire sanctification. Yet, he believed that God manifested in power as recorded in the book of Acts. Moved by the stories circulating from Indonesia, Bustin went to experience firsthand the revival fires that were spreading through the remote villages and various islands around Indonesia. His experiences are recorded in a small book called, *Dead: Yet ... Live*.[109] Bustin spread the message of holiness among the Timorese people, but he also became an advocate of the *charismata* as a normative expression within Spirit-filled people. He wrote, "If God is unchangeable, and if we believe that the blessed Holy Spirit still operates in His Church today, we should expect to see evidences of the supernatural even in signs and wonders in our day."[110]

I believe that Bustin's theology was biblically centered. He embraced and taught a theology of purity and power. However, he was not well received by many in the Holiness movement upon his return to the United States in the early 1970s, and in fact, he was criticized and branded a fabricator among his own people and among those in various evangelical and holiness camps. Bustin was accepted as long as he taught sanctification merely as a doctrine, but when he taught sanctification as an experience that is exemplified in charismatic activity, problems began to ensue. Bustin found he soon joined the ranks of those, who like Wesley, were criticized for actually believing the Bible.

Many evangelicals seem to join Bishop Butler's rebuke of John Wesley: "Sir the pretending to extraordinary revelations and gifts of the Holy Ghost is a horrid thing, a very horrid thing."[111] Ruthven asked a simple question: "What is the reason for such revulsion to contemporary charismatic experience?"[112] I believe a number of responses could be given in answer to this question, such as inappropriate or unscriptural displays of the *charismata,* an overemphasis on the *charismata,* fear and ignorance about the subject of the *charismata,* or simply a theological box, which does not permit the *charismata.* Ruthven's own response was that within Christian theology, miracles have come to signify the additional revelation of qualitatively new Christian doctrine. In other words, the *charismata* incite fear in people because they believe new content is being added to the Scriptures. This, of course, is due to an ignorance of the New Testament emphasis—a problem that we've already discussed.

There might be another response as to why there seems to be such an outcry to the display of charismatic power. Miracles establish a line of demarcation, forcing us to choose on which side of the line we will stand. A lifestyle of signs and wonders challenges those who are content to live without them. It once was stated that "powerlessness is such an aberration that we are either compelled to seek for a fresh baptism in the Spirit until the power that was promised becomes manifested through us, or we create doctrinal reasons to comfort ourselves in powerlessness."[113] Many have chosen to rewrite theologies and doctrines that dismiss the value or necessity of the *charismata,* simply because they do not want to inconvenience themselves for a fresh touch of God's Spirit.

Recently I was talking with Craig Rench, a Nazarene pastor, and learned of a group of Christians in China who are fasting and praying with great fervency because they fear they have lost their anointing. When I asked how they made such an assessment, Craig responded that this group of Christians was only seeing one person raised from the dead per month, and they were used to seeing more. Therefore, they thought it necessary to inconvenience themselves for a renewed touch by God.

These kinds of activities cannot be limited to China or Third World areas; they must become normative in Christians everywhere. However, in order for a theology to embrace these kinds of activities, there must be a sincere desire and effort to pursue God with a ceaseless passion. Spiritual apathy can *never* be tolerated if we want a theology inclusive of charismatic activity. If there is not a sincere effort or willingness to chase after God for fresh encounters, we might even question one's theology of salvation.

I've come across those who inadvertently believe that once they have experienced entire sanctification or a purified heart, they no longer require anything more from God. However, that mindset simply is not true. There is always more of God for us to receive. My challenge to everyone who is reading this book is that we live with a perpetual hunger for more: more grace, more love, more faith, more power, and more of the Spirit. Jesus told us in the context of prayer that the Father would give us more of the Holy Spirit if we asked (Luke 11:13; John 3:34). The Bible says that God wants us to be in an ongoing state of "being filled" (present-tense verb) with the Holy Spirit (Eph. 5:18). The believers in the book of Acts received a fresh impartation of the Holy Spirit about four years after Pentecost (Acts 4:31) and continued to be filled with the Holy Spirit (Acts 13:52). We have the privilege and the responsibility to increase in truth and grace just like Jesus did (Luke 2:52). In light of these Scriptures, if we are not functioning in charismatic power, we need to continue our pursuit of God until this power is normative. It should become normative; we cannot allow ourselves to become content and cease pursuing God. Every day that we're alive should be another day of moving closer to Him.

There is another implication to developing a theology of the Word and the Spirit: Bible schools and seminaries will need to evaluate what they consider "academic excellence." Certainly diplomas should be awarded for those who achieve specific criteria, but inclusive to Bible knowledge, exams, and term papers, there should be an understanding, and a practicum, of deploying spiritual gifts. Bible classes should be arranged around learning to hear the prophetic words of the Spirit who speaks through Spirit-filled vessels (Acts 2:17). As stated previously, theology must be practical. Theology is never more practical than when it equips students with spiritual gifts and then sends them out to utilize those gifts in the marketplace.

There is one final implication to consider in developing a biblical emphasis. Churches (denominations, and specifically the Holiness movement) will need to consider developing a curriculum that instructs God's people in the Word and the Spirit. Discipleship within the local church will need to look more like a rabbinic style of mentorship where we do not merely teach the Bible in a classroom, but we take new believers into the community—prophesying, praying for the sick, leading people to Christ, or simply encouraging the broken hearted. Simply stated, discipleship programs within the Church will need to be inclusive of the fruit of the Spirit *and* the gifts of the Spirit. The combination of the Word and the Spirit was in the heart of Wesley and his band of Methodists, and those components comprised the DNA of the Holiness movement. Hopefully, we have not strayed too far from our roots. Many churches and denominations have already started the process of rebuilding a theology inclusive of Word and Spirit. My prayer is that the remarriage will occur in my lifetime.

Chapter Seven

The Two-Winged Dove

—◦◦◦—

R eplicating Jesus cannot be properly experienced if purity
and power remain separated, and we certainly won't
accomplish much for the kingdom if they remain apart. I
appreciate the attempts that have been made in bringing
purity and power together, but it is not enough for the two
concepts to simply abide together or hold hands as friends.
The divorce must end and a remarriage must be established.
We must experience a one-flesh union with purity and power
as observed in the Wesleyan crusades. For that matter, we
need only to look to Jesus' life and ministry throughout the
Scriptures to see a model of purity and power working in
perfect Spirit-led unity.

The Bible says that Jesus was full of grace and truth (John
1:14). First, He operated full of grace meaning that Jesus
was filled with God's divine influence: the power and favor
of God. Grace is so extraordinary that Paul declared we are
saved because of it (Eph. 2:8). Grace is more than unmerited
favor; it is a divine *force* that levels mountains (Zech. 4:7)
and redeems, heals, delivers, and restores our lives to spiritual vitality. Without grace, spiritual gifts (*charismata*) would
not be active. The root word for gifts is grace (*charis*), and
grace makes the gifts operative in our lives. Jesus was full of

grace, and His lifestyle demonstrated that grace as He traveled about and healed all kinds of sickness and disease among the people (Matt. 4:23–24).

Second, Jesus was full of truth. He did not come to destroy the Law but rather to fulfill it (Matt. 5:17). His life, integrity, and morality were impeccable; He was the unblemished Lamb of God: the great High Priest who was tempted in every way, yet without sin (Heb. 4:15). Jesus was the embodiment of truth and righteousness. He was the only person capable of throwing stones at a sinful woman caught in adultery because He stood before her in total holiness, yet He was the only one who could pardon her and set the standard for moral purity. Jesus was the fusion of grace and truth, of purity and power.

Additionally, Jesus' commission accounts involved this perfect blend; He sent His disciples out to preach the Word, and it was to be followed by supernatural activity. His lifestyle was the marriage of character and *charismata,* the perfect integration of how we should move and have our being. Jesus' challenge to the religious leaders underscored the fact that they didn't have a clue about this divine union when He told them they were going astray for not knowing the Scriptures or the power of God (Matt. 22:29). Grace and truth, Word and Spirit, purity and power: these aspects were uniquely joined in the life of Jesus, and they must be replicated by His followers.

Fruits and Functions

There is an interesting fusion between the fruits of the Spirit and the functions (manifestations or gifts) of the Spirit in the Bible. Both, the fruits and the functions, are the result of the activity of the Holy Spirit in our life. Most people understand the fruits of the Spirit (Gal. 5:22–23) as characteristics that grow and mature over time once we are filled with the Spirit. It wouldn't be inaccurate to suggest that these fruits grow best out of a pure heart (a life spent walking in the Spirit and obeying His direct revelation). The context for Paul's discussion of these nine fruits is the crucifying of the flesh and our constant abiding in the Spirit. Chances are slim that an impure, self-centered, carnal believer will manifest love, joy, peace, longsuffering, and so on, very well. So I'm suggesting that a pure heart will grow fruit.

The functions of the Spirit are also discussed by Paul as the activity of the Holy Spirit (1 Cor. 12:7–10). There are nine supernatural gifts that Paul identified that are poured out through a Spirit-filled believer. While we can mature through the Spirit in the execution of these nine gifts, they are not the result of our own efforts; in other words, unlike the fruits, the gifts are not grown. These gifts are the supernatural result of the Spirit's power activated through us, and they are necessary to edify and profit the entire body of Christ (1 Cor. 12:7; 14:12). We can conclude that the fruits grow out of purity and the functions are given as a result of power.

The problem arises when we attempt to argue the value of each. What is of more value, the fruits or the functions of the Spirit? When we try to underscore one over the other, the schism ensues. I agree with Jack Hayford's statement, "I doubt God would concur with our ever-imposing competing priorities where He has not proposed or forced a choice. Nothing in the Word of God indicates that either character or *charismata* is preferred or deferred by Him. Rather, the Holy Spirit is calling us all to move in both today."[114] I would make a strong case biblically that the fruits and functions are of equal value, and both are the result of the same Holy Spirit filling us. It has been a tragic mistake to dissect the Spirit and divide His operations as history reveals that we have done.

The Holy Spirit as a Dove

In John 1:32, John observed that the Holy Spirit descended upon Jesus like a dove. Many churches around the world have rightly used the dove as a symbol for the Holy Spirit. I once heard Leonard Ravenhill speak about a dove having nine specific bones and feathers comprising each wing, and he suggested that one wing represents the nine fruits and the other wing, the nine gifts. I'm certainly not an ornithologist, but I know a dove can't fly if it loses one wing.

I don't mean to sound critical, but too many churches and denominations within the Holiness movement, even in Pentecostal and Charismatic circles, are flopping around and floundering on the ground because we have dissected the Holy Spirit and exonerated power or purity over the other. It's unbiblical to separate the work of God in that manner, and it has caused its share of problems over the years. We will always stray into tributaries if we emphasize one over the other.

Consider, for example, holiness churches that have taught sanctification (purity) without including the manifesting power of the Spirit, particularly in charismatic functions. Growing up in a holiness church, I can attest that many in my tribe steered clear of teaching sanctification in conjunction with the empowering work of the Holy Spirit that was demonstrated in a supernatural lifestyle expressed in the *charismata*. I cannot recall a single message while growing up that addressed how holiness could be expressed through casting out demons, prophesying, healing the sick, or speaking words of knowledge. Sanctification was more about avoiding "things" than actually "doing things," namely, doing ministry under the influence of the Spirit's power.

Worse still, in the attempt to emphasize purity as a greater component to the Spirit's baptism than power, many of our churches have fallen prey to the apostle Paul's warning of "having a form of godliness but denying its power" (2 Tim.

3:5). To "deny" here literally means to disavow or to break ties with something that you once embraced. Paul was talking about believers who deny the message of godliness its power (*dunamis*). So we settle for the structure or shape of godliness, but we break ties with the miraculous power of the Holy Spirit. Godliness without power is religious, hollow, and superficial at best. I've read the early accounts of the Methodists and the Nazarenes and many other groups in the Holiness movement, who preached purity and demonstrated power. Godliness was once associated with an extraordinary anointing and a spiritual fervency. But these days, too many believers have pushed the supernatural power of the Spirit out of their churches and opted for a lifeless substitute for holiness. When a person is sanctified and filled with the Holy Spirit, the Spirit should manifest through them for the health and edification of the body of Christ. We should not fear, grieve, or quench the Holy Spirit's miraculous activity that He desires to manifest through us.

Moreover, if we divorce ourselves from the supernatural power of God as expressed in this verse, we will open the door to *other* powers that are not of God. Paul mentioned Jannes and Jambres resisting Moses in the same context of denying power (2 Tim. 3:8). The enemy came into the courts of Pharaoh, using sorcery and divination to resist and mock Moses. The power of God was much greater, however, than the demonic ploys, and Moses prevailed. Redemption came to God's people because the power of God was manifested. Can you imagine what the enemy will do in our churches if we reject the power of God? What protection will we have? I've met and ministered in holiness churches where too many people were bound by demonic strongholds. Usually they are a part of churches that have denied or resisted the power of the Holy Spirit. Our only chance of remaining in victory over the enemy is through the power of God (Eph. 6:10).

Additionally, preaching a form of godliness without power will inevitably drift toward legalism. Few would deny that the Holiness movement tragically complicated the preaching of sanctification with rules and regulations that replaced a life of true holiness. During the middle of the twentieth century, holiness churches formed what Dunn described as "boundary markers; superficial practices that reinforce the sense of distinctive identity of a particular group."[115] Boundary markers for the Jews became circumcision, dietary laws, and Sabbath keeping. It wasn't long until the Pharisees associated who was "in" their particular group, based on these practices. Jesus cautioned them about invalidating the Word of God in favor of their traditions handed down by their fathers (Mark 7:13). The Holiness movement had its own share of boundary markers over the years, and we most certainly knew who was in our particular group of the sanctified. Adherence to our specific practices perpetuated a sectarian mindset that created much tension between "us and them."

We seemed to tolerate a lot of carnality under the guise of "holiness" in our movement. As long as we knew how to dress and to avoid various types of jewelry, we were part of the sanctified club. We knew where to go and where not to go, what to say and what not to say. I witnessed an almost smug pride in some of our holiness folks because of the rules that they kept with strict adherence. This description is certainly not true of everyone within the Holiness movement. Many experienced the liberating joy and supernatural power in being sanctified. I can, unfortunately, remember too many legalistic boundary markers that defined sanctification. Amidst our rule-keeping, we often failed to ponder whether we exemplified Jesus in His love or His lifestyle.

When the message of sanctification is distilled down to rule-keeping and good ethics, we also fail to emphasize being "set apart" for a priestly function. Among other things, sanctification means that we are set apart to be a holy priesthood

(1 Pet. 2:9). Sanctification in the New Testament is accompanied by the Holy Spirit—the Spirit of revelation—who enables believers to hear and deliver the Word of God (Isa. 59:21). Growing up in the holiness church, I was not taught that being "holy" meant that we could speak prophetically into our generation. Moreover, I didn't hear that being sanctified meant that I was empowered to replicate Jesus' works. In all of our rules and regulations, somehow (willingly or by negligence) we failed to emphasize the importance of obeying the components of the commissioning accounts that commanded us to heal the sick, cleanse the lepers, and raise the dead—doing the things Jesus actually did.

On the other side of the camp, however, is a group of churches committed to experiencing the power of the Holy Spirit, while simultaneously downplaying the necessity of purity. We've already discussed how the Pentecostal movement overlooked sanctification in favor of speaking in tongues as well as other manifestations. Emphasizing the manifestations of the Spirit without a foundation of holiness is not only unbiblical, it's destructive.

One only needs to take a brief cursory scan of the Corinthian believers to see what a movement looks like when it is drawn to the supernatural but lacks holiness. Paul was hindered to speak to these believers about the supernatural (the meaning of spiritual, *pneumatikos,* in 1 Cor. 3:1) because of their lack of purity and unity. These Christians made their way out of paganism, but it seems those practices never made their way out of these Christians. They were divisive, contentious, and self-centered. Before Paul's elaborate discussion of the *charismata* in chapter twelve of Corinthians, he disciplined them for their factions and schisms. "I do not praise you, since you come together not for the better but for the worse" (1 Cor. 11:17). That indictment is a commentary on any church that lacks holiness. The manifestation of the Spirit is given to profit the Church (1 Cor. 12:7), but there will be no lasting benefit to the Spirit's graces when we deemphasize a holy lifestyle that emerges from a pure heart.

Recently, I was having breakfast with a prominent Charismatic pastor in southern California. He's an apostolic leader and is well respected by many who know him. We talked about various aspects of ministry before our conversation turned toward the subject of holiness. It wasn't long into our discussion when his eyes filled with tears as he explained how many of his people were able to prophesy and flow in supernatural power, yet they lacked the integrity and the character associated with sanctification. A similar story was told to me by a friend who is a pastor on staff at a Charismatic church in Ohio. He said me, "Our people know how to operate with the gifts at church, but they lack holiness in the way they treat each other in the parking lot." I wish these conversations were isolated reports, but if the truth is known, I've heard this same kind of lament from many leaders in Charismatic and Pentecostal churches.

J. Lee Grady, contributing editor of *Charisma* magazine, recently came to the conclusion that the Charismatic movement was all but dead. "What began as a dynamic explosion of the Holy Spirit's life and power," wrote Grady, "has become increasingly shallow. The tide has gone out, leaving on the shore all kinds of debris."[116] Among the reasons for his diagnosis, Grady believes that many within American Charismatic/Pentecostal churches are carnal and self-centered. He writes candidly of problems surfacing in the church like immorality, defiled altars, a lack of integrity, and greasy grace, calling Charismatics to "a fresh baptism of purity."[117] Grady wrote with passion and concern for a people he loves so dearly who, in his opinion, desperately need holiness.

DeArteaga came to the same conclusions after reviewing a series of scandals surrounding some of the more famous Charismatic leaders during the 1980s. The disparaging fallout of these leaders was sad and disappointing for all, regardless the tribe to which we belong. DeArteaga suggested several factors for the demise, such as the decline of the Lord's Supper as a place for encountering the transforming presence of God, the rejection of Methodist/Holiness codes of conduct in fear of legalism, and rejection of deeper levels of accountability among believers as seen in classical Methodism. In his final analysis, he stated, "This steady stream of fraudulent actions, excessive luxury, and sexual immorality ... should warn us that something important is missing from American Christian spirituality (specifically in the Charismatic movement)."[118] What *is* missing? DeArteaga answered that question by stating that beyond having a born-again experience, "many Christians do not follow-up (the born-again experience) with persistent seeking after holiness."[119] Churches should not divorce themselves from the necessity of holiness and purity of heart. Purity and power as the two-winged dove cannot be impaired in any fashion.

To dissect the Holy Spirit in favor of purity or power is a mistreatment of His presence, and it's something that I don't want to be a part of. Consider for a moment the many ways we can mistreat the Holy Spirit. We can blaspheme the Spirit (Matt. 12:31), we can lie to the Spirit (Acts 5:3), we can test the Spirit (Acts 5:9), we can resist the Spirit (Acts 7:51), we can grieve the Spirit (Eph. 4:30), we can reject the Spirit (1 Thess. 4:8), we can quench the Spirit (1 Thess. 5:18), and we can insult the Spirit (Heb. 10:29). If we prohibit the Dove (Holy Spirit) from operating with both wings or if we attempt to magnify one wing over the other, I believe we are treating God's Spirit inappropriately and will stand accountable before Him for such actions. It is time to let the Dove fly as it was created to do with both wings; we must let the Holy Spirit operate in purity and power, in fruits and functions.

The Genesis of the Dove

The Bible begins with an interesting fusion of the Word and the Spirit working in congruency. In Genesis 1:1–3, the Spirit of God was hovering over the face of the waters. Some have translated "waters" as chaos. We also learn from this passage that the earth was without form and void. Without "form" also means confusion and chaos, and being "void" means desolate and empty. In the midst of this condition we discover the Spirit was brooding as a bird would do over her unhatched eggs. Birds wait with anticipation when brooding for what is about to transpire; they rest over the potential life that is about to spring forth. Brooding over the face of the waters, as we see in this Genesis account, was also an act of preparation. The Spirit (i.e., Dove) was incubating the elements in preparation for God to speak. In other words, the elements were ready to hear the spoken Word of God because of the activity of the Spirit.

In this Genesis account, it seems that the Spirit was waiting for the Word of God to be declared. Think about it, the Spirit was brooding over chaos, confusion, desolation, and emptiness waiting for what God was about to release. I would like to suggest that the Spirit knew *exactly* what was about to be released, and because of that expectation, the Spirit was anticipating the life—the order—that was forthcoming in the midst of that darkness and chaos. The Spirit's excitement rested in the Word of God because the Spirit knew what God's Word was capable of doing—what it is capable of bringing to life.

Who gets excited in the midst of darkness and chaos? The Holy Spirit! When does God speak forth His Word? Often in the middle of chaos after the Holy Spirit has been brooding! The Word and the Spirit cooperated here in Genesis—it's a picture of the two-winged Dove. Regardless of how chaotic or messy the circumstances are in our lives, if the Spirit of God and the Word of God are cooperating, something is going to get created.

This same pattern was evident in Ezekiel 37 when the priest was brought to a valley filled with dry bones and as he looked over the situation, he observed the fact that the bones were many and they were dry. The desolation of this scene looked familiar to the barren and chaotic mess in Genesis 1:2. God told Ezekiel to prophesy to the bones, and that was exactly what he did. The Word of God was spoken over the dry heap, but in order for those bones to live, something else needed to occur. God commanded Ezekiel to speak to the breath (*ruach*), a word which refers to the Spirit of God. The breath, or the Spirit, came into those bones, and they lived, they stood, and they became an exceedingly great army. Once again there is a congruency between the Word and the Spirit functioning together to bring order, life, purpose, and creation.

I believe this is why Paul said, "For our gospel did not come to you in word only, but also in power, and in the Holy Spirit" (1 Thess. 1:3). The gospel produced order, life, and purpose among the Thessalonians because it was a gospel of the Word and the Spirit. Paul alluded to the same thing in 1 Corinthians 2:4 when he said that his preaching was not with words only, but a demonstration of the Spirit in power. Paul's ministry report from the city of Illyricum involved the presentation of the gospel through "word and deed" (Rom. 15:18). He preached the Word of God, and the Spirit showed up with mighty signs and wonders.

In the book of Acts, we find a young church undergoing persecution. These early Christians were being threatened by religious and political powers. Rather than cower in the face of this threat, these believers called for a prayer meeting. Guess what they asked God for? They wanted to preach God's Word with greater boldness, and they also wanted God to stretch out His hand and perform signs and wonders (Acts 4:29). I propose to you that these believers wanted the two-winged

Dove to function within the Church. In the midst of darkness, in the midst of adversity and persecution, the answer would come in the Word and the Spirit working with congruency.

Ending the Divorce

When the believers were baptized with the Holy Spirit at Pentecost, two corresponding experiences occurred. First, they were purified (see Acts 15:8–9), and second, they were given power (see Acts 1:8). In other words, they were made holy, *and* they were enabled to operate in charismatic ministry; both results demonstrated the fullness of the Holy Spirit in their lives. That experience is the present activity of the Holy Spirit in our lives when we are baptized with Him, and we simply must not divorce this two-fold function any longer. The Holy Spirit purifies our heart, and the same Spirit anoints us with power; this is a biblical union.

When my wife and I were married many years ago, we had no intentions of separating. We made a vow before God and people that our union would last a lifetime. On that day, our journey began and regardless of the difficulties and challenges we've endured, we have slowly fused our lives together in the passing of time to the point of inseparability. Yes, there are unique differences that we each have, but together we are one flesh—just as God designed it to be. Additionally, our union has birthed blessings: namely, children and grandchildren.

My prayer is that we will treat purity and power (or Word and Spirit) as a biblical marriage that must endure for all seasons of life. I pray that we will no longer divide into camps, looking smugly over the fence at "those people." God designed purity and power to share a divine romance—to function as one flesh accomplishing kingdom endeavors. I realize that each component brings something different to the relationship, and I've attempted to emphasize the necessity for both. We need the Word of God preached; we need people of character and holiness. Purity of heart is essential, and we dare not diminish that work. We also need to function in the power of the Spirit; we need the gifts and graces that the Spirit brings. But it's time to re-marry the two components. Yes, there will be challenges along the way, and we'll need to work through our differences. It will be worth it, however, because the marriage of purity and power, the union of Word and Spirit, will produce blessings for generations to come. A way in which to marry these two concepts is through discipling people. I realize many Christian truths should be conveyed when mentoring believers, but we certainly *must* include the activities that Jesus emphasized with His own disciples that were characterized in the book of Acts. Let's look at discipleship in the supernatural.

Chapter Eight

Discipleship in the Supernatural

———❦———

I n Pilot Point, Texas, in 1908, the Church of the Nazarene was formally organized, bringing together the purity of the Wesleyan Holiness movement as well as the power for service from the result of being baptized in the Holy Spirit. The Church of the Nazarene was birthed in purity and power, and it resembled the early Church in the book of Acts. In fact, the manual for the Church of the Nazarene presently states, "The Church of the Nazarene ... seeks the simplicity and spiritual power manifest in the primitive New Testament Church."[120] Among other things, our church desires to imitate the believers in the book of Acts who, within seventy years, influenced, touched, and transformed more than one-million people amidst Roman tyranny. Their effectiveness in seeing spiritual transformation was because they *manifested* power.

Let's be honest, many discipleship programs scarcely talk about the subject matter of imitating the New Testament Church in charismatic power. I believe many subjects can and should be taught when mentoring others, but we cannot avoid instructing people in the kinds of activities that the primitive New Testament believers functioned in, especially since we say that we *seek* that spiritual power. Have you ever noted the power evidenced in these primitive believers? It's extraordinary to say the least. Consider the following:

> And they continued in the apostles' doctrine and fellowship, in the breaking of bread, and in prayers. Then fear came upon every soul, and many wonders and signs were done through the apostles. (Acts 2:42–43)

> Then Peter said, "Silver and gold I do not have, but what I do have I give to you; In the name of Jesus Christ of Nazareth, rise up and walk." (Acts 3:6)

> And with great power the apostles gave witness to the resurrection and of the Lord Jesus. And great grace was upon them all. (Acts 4:33)

> And through the hands of the apostles many signs and wonders were done among the people…so that they brought the sick out into the streets and laid them on beds and couches, that at least the shadow of Peter passing by might fall on some of them. Also a multitude gathered from the surrounding cities to Jerusalem, bringing sick people and those who were tormented by unclean spirits, and they were all healed. (Acts 5:12, 15–16)

> And Stephen, full of faith and power, did great wonders and signs among the people. (Acts 6:8)

> Then Philip went down to the city of Samaria and preached Christ to them. And the

multitudes with one accord heeded the things spoken by Philip, hearing and seeing the miracles which he did. (Acts 8:5–6)

But Peter put them all out, and knelt down and prayed. And turning to the body he said, "Tabitha, arise." And she opened her eyes, and when she saw Peter she sat up. (Acts 9:40).

Then one of them, named Agabus, stood up and showed by the Spirit that there was going to be a great famine throughout all the world. (Acts 11:28)

Then all the multitudes kept silent and listened to Barnabas and Paul declaring how many miracles and wonders God had worked through them among the Gentiles. (Acts 15:12)

Now God worked unusual miracles by the hands of Paul, so that even handkerchiefs or aprons were brought from his body to the sick, and the diseases left them and the evil spirits went out of them. (Acts 19:11–12)

And it happened that the father of Publius lay sick of a fever and dysentery. Paul went in to him and prayed, and he laid his hands on him and healed him. So when this was done, the rest of those on the island who had diseases also came and were healed. (Acts 28:8–9)

If these experiences are the kinds of activities that we say we are seeking to imitate, then we should consider discipleship methods that not only discuss this kind of power, but deploy believers into a world equipped to function like these early believers. This type of power has been termed "effective" power, a power that made a difference; a power to bring wholeness of mind, of body, and of spiritual relationships.[121] So I'm suggesting that discipleship strategies must include instruction and application of this kind of power. Otherwise, we are falling short of seeking the power manifested in the primitive New Testament Church. The activities demonstrated in the book of Acts were initiated by Jesus when He deployed His disciples. Jesus demonstrated a supernatural lifestyle, equipped His followers to imitate Him, and then dispersed them into a world stuffed with the power of the Holy Spirit to accomplish their mission on earth. Therefore, our strategy for discipling believers and equipping them to evangelize should model Jesus' approach.

In addition, discipleship strategies must extend beyond theory and talk. Jesus demonstrated a lifestyle of supernatural activity before His followers, and then He sent them out to "do the works." Too many traditional discipleship programs center on the instruction aspect, but participant activation, where students actually do the works of Jesus, is significantly lacking. What often happens is participants are able to recite creeds and doctrines central to the movement, but they know little of the *charismata* or actually how to deploy these gifts in the marketplace (not to mention within the walls of the church). Randy Clark accurately wrote:

> Discipleship is more than observing—watching, viewing, scrutinizing, monitoring, studying, examining, surveying—it is becoming like the teacher by doing what one is told. This is the root of our theological education problem. We have mistaken *studying the Master* for *becoming like Him*. We have mistaken *observing* for *doing*. We

> have replaced the Jewish understanding of
> discipleship with a Greek understanding. The
> New Testament was written by Jews, with a
> Jewish understanding of discipleship, not with
> a Greek understanding. [122]

I never felt more equipped to be like Jesus than when I spent a day with someone as they ministered to people in the marketplace. I watched as this person interacted with strangers, and I was intrigued by how they demonstrated Christ. Their goal was not to speak the gospel but to *be* the gospel. The motivating factor for them while ministering was to express divine love, and God's love seemed to open the door to the activity of the Spirit. By the end of the day, after watching my friend pray with people or prophesy to them or speak words of knowledge into them, I felt more equipped to live like Jesus in my world.

What I'm going to describe is an aspect of discipleship that integrates the supernatural gifts. I said earlier that I was going to swing the pendulum just a bit toward the activity of the Holy Spirit because of the target audience of this book. For clarification and emphasis, let me state that when I teach discipleship in the course, *Living in the Supernatural* (*LS*), included in the curriculum is a section that comprehensively covers holiness and heart purity. To assist with further clarification, I have included a brief outline of *LS* in the appendix of this book. Let's take a look at the supernatural gifts and how they might be deployed through Spirit-filled believers.

Understanding the Supernatural Gifts

One of the most prominent theologians in the Church of the Nazarene was the late H. Orton Wiley (1877–1961). Encouraged by the denomination, he wrote his "magnum opus," a three-volume systematic theology. Concerning spiritual gifts, Wiley stated:

> The gifts of the Spirit are essential to the spiritual progress of the Church … the spiritual mission of the Church can be carried forward only by spiritual means … it is evident that the gifts of the Spirit are always latent in the Church. They did not cease with the apostles, but are available to the Church in every age.[123]

Spiritual gifts are essential, and the spiritual progress of the Church simply will not occur without the deployment of the *charismata*. Note Wiley's last sentence, "gifts did not cease with the apostles." If they didn't cease with the apostles, we must develop discipleship curriculum that talks about the gifts of the Spirit. We must train believers how to function with gifts as normative behavior for all Spirit-filled people.

To be fair, there have been a number of books and resources published over the years within the Holiness movement concerning spiritual gifts. But I have not discovered many that teach believers how to deploy those gifts. Also, I'm not talking about the abilities listed in Romans 12:3–8 or the assignments listed in Ephesians 4:11. I'm talking about the nine supernatural gifts in 1 Corinthians 12:8–10. The Corinthian list of gifts is different in nature; they are the "manifestations" (*phanerosis*, the display, exhibition, or expression) of the Spirit (1 Cor. 12:7). Simply put, if a believer is filled with the Spirit, they will potentially be a candidate to operate in the nine functions however the Spirit desires to display those functions in the life of the believer. I realize that this suggestion cuts against the grain of long-held beliefs about the gifts. For years, I was taught that I possessed at least one or more of the gifts. But the emphasis in this passage (1 Cor. 12:8–10) is not so much about the gift as it is a manifestation. In other words, the list in Corinthians is not about gifts that we possess; these gifts are the result of *being* possessed, namely, by the Holy Spirit.

The manifestation of the Spirit, as the whole, is of greater concern to Paul than the actual display of individual graces. The real emphasis behind the Corinthian list of charismatic activities is on the Spirit Himself, and the Spirit displays Himself not for the benefit of the individual believer, but for the entire assembly. Gordon Fee said that the Corinthian list is a "disclosure of the Spirit's activity" in the midst of God's people.[124] The Spirit is on display, in other words, and we are the canvas or instrument that He uses. Each one of us, when filled with the Spirit, becomes the tool that the Spirit uses to edify the Church.

The fact is all of us can be filled with the Holy Spirit. And once possessed by the Spirit, extraordinary activities can occur through any of us. This concept is the meaning behind the word "spiritual" used by Paul (1 Cor. 12:1). This word "spiritual" (*pneumatikos*) means supernatural activities in this context. When we are Spirit-filled and Spirit-led, we become the instrument through whom supernatural activities can go on display (manifest). Paul identified nine specific activities, noting that it is the Spirit working all of these manifestations as He wills (1 Cor. 12:11).

Let's look a bit closer at this verse, "But one and the same Spirit works all these things, distributing to each one individually as He wills" (1 Cor. 12:11). The Spirit distributes to each person the particular manifestation that He wills. The word *distributes* means to divide out or to pour through, and it's a present-tense verb. So the idea behind this word is that the Spirit continually pours through each of us (manifests) in a manner that pleases Him and in a way that builds up the body of Christ. These manifestations are not about us. They have little to do with us; we're merely the vessel that the Spirit uses for the entire assembly.

I have been gardening for many years and have a very large garden at our house. Stretched out from the house is a one-hundred-foot garden hose, and at the end of this hose is an expensive nozzle. This nozzle is capable of applying water in a variety of ways depending on the kind of plant that I want to nurture. This nozzle can offer a mist, a shower, or a soaking, and so on, for a total of nine different functions, depending on the size and needs of the plant I'm watering. All I need to do is click the end of the nozzle for a different distribution—manifestation—of water. It's the same water source, but the way I adjust the nozzle determines how the water flows out.

We are like this nozzle, and the Holy Spirit is the source that flows through each of us. Who determines how the Spirit flows out of us? The Spirit of God does, to each one individually as He wills. If the Spirit wants to manifest through a word of knowledge, He adjusts us for that application. If the Spirit wants to manifest through miracles, He adjusts us to produce those results. He can even flow all nine manifestations through us in one occasion if He so desires. We belong to Him to be used for His purposes. These are not *our* gifts to wield as we desire; these nine manifestations are the workings of the Spirit for His cause.

Therefore, at any given moment in a corporate gathering, the Holy Spirit may use me in a manner that is very different from the way He uses you. In the next gathering, it will look entirely different. There have been services where I was given prophetic words for people while others manifested healing gifts. The next night, I was used by God to distribute healing gifts while my ministry companions functioned in prophetic words. So there were diversity of activities, but the same God worked all of these things in each of us (1 Cor. 12:6). The idea of a "fixed" gift that we all possess is not what Paul was describing in Corinth. Therefore, when he asked the rhetorical questions are all workers of miracles? Do all have gifts of healings? Do all speak in tongues (1 Cor. 12:29–30)? The correct answer is no, usually not at the same time. Why? It is because the Spirit is adjusting each of us, individually, in a variety of ways—as He wills—to release His presence upon people.

But what if God uses a person in only *one* manifestation for an extended period of time? Then that person should not compare themselves with another person in the body of Christ. The "foot" shouldn't compare itself to the "hand," or the "head" to the "feet" (1 Cor. 12:16, 21). Members of the body of Christ shouldn't be insecure or arrogant with the particular manifestation that is operating through them regardless of how frequent or infrequent the manifestation lasts. It's not about the individual; it's about the welfare of the entire body. Therefore, we view all members and manifestations in the body of Christ as necessary; we esteem the weak, and we encourage the spiritually immature (1 Cor. 12:23–24), so that the Church is edified (1 Cor. 14:12).

When the Spirit is leading and using us, all things will be done decently and in order (1 Cor. 14:40). There will be no schisms; members will care for one another, support one another, and honor one another (1 Cor. 12:25–26). The Church will be edified, and in that kind of Spirit-anointed atmosphere, unbelievers will be convinced and convicted by all (1 Cor. 14:24). That scriptural description is a picture of a church functioning in purity and power—a Word and Spirit church—a body of believers where the Holy Spirit is free to operate through biblically centered, sanctified vessels. I believe that description should be emphasized in all discipleship programs.

The Nine Manifestations

To really understand the nine manifestations that Paul listed, let's briefly explore the passage in the broader context.

114

The narrative begins at 1 Corinthians 11:17 and concludes at 1 Corinthians 14:40. These two passages are like bookends to a supernatural culture. At the beginning of this narrative, Paul was very distraught with the church of Corinth. He stated, "Now in giving these instructions I do not praise you, since you come together not for the better but for the worse" (1 Cor. 11:17). The gathering of this church produced injurious and ill effects; the people were selfish and divisive. At the end of the narrative Paul wrote, "Let all things be done decently and in order" (1 Cor. 14:40). The words *decently* and *order* describe something that has been carefully arranged, much like puzzle pieces that when fitted together, produce a beautiful picture.

So Paul began with an injurious, hurtful church and ended up talking about a church that was arranged and beautifully shaped—a "glorious" church (Eph. 5:27). In order to get from the starting point to the ending point, we obviously have to walk through three essential chapters of directives which are as follows: general instructions about manifestations (chap. 12), manifestations rooted in divine love (chap. 13), and appropriate use of manifestations in the assembly (chap. 14). No doubt, the issue for Corinth was the inappropriate use of tongues in the assembly, which warranted strong exhortations by Paul. Interestingly, tongues are still a source of dissention among believers. Churches of all denominations would do well to read and adhere to Paul's instructions in the fourteenth chapter of Corinthians.

There are many ways the nine manifestations can be arranged in terms of grouping. I choose to group them in three categories: prophetic manifestations (prophecy, word of wisdom, word of knowledge, discerning of spirits), power manifestations (faith, healing, miracles), and proclamation manifestations (tongues, interpretation of tongues). Let's look briefly at these manifestations.

Prophetic Manifestations

1. Prophecy (*prophetea*)

This gift is a divine utterance; a discourse or message that is given to us by divine inspiration. In the context, Paul is describing *forth-telling* (a message of hope, encouragement) more than *foretelling* (predicting the future). When we prophesy to someone, the words that we speak bring edification, exhortation, and comfort to them (1 Cor. 14:3). What we speak is known only by hearing the Lord speak to us, so we are declaring something that has been given to us by the Holy Spirit. All Christians hear His voice (John 10:27), so if we hear His voice we can speak what He says.

The gift of prophecy is so helpful to the body of Christ that Paul said we should especially desire this manifestation more than the others (1 Cor. 14:1). Moreover, Peter said that when the Holy Spirit is poured out on all flesh, one of the blessings of that outpouring will be the ability to prophesy (Acts 2:17). The key to this particular gift is intimacy with Jesus; learning to live in union with the Spirit so that we can speak in the Spirit. We'll talk more about this lifestyle in the next chapter.

Some people identify and limit this gift to preaching. That understanding of prophecy certainly is plausible. Hopefully, when a preacher is speaking to a congregation, he or she is speaking under divine influence. But prophecy goes beyond preaching to include speaking *into* someone words specifically meant for that person. We might hear a Scripture verse, an encouraging word, or even a descriptive message for or about a person. Jesus demonstrated this function when He spoke to the woman at the well about her assortment of husbands, and those words so inspired her that many Samaritans believed in Jesus because of this woman's testimony about Jesus' prophetic words (John 4:39).

2. Word of Wisdom (*sophia*)

Wisdom is supreme insight; a spiritual insight that is given by God. Wisdom is to be sought after according to many of the Proverbs. James said that if any of us lacks wisdom, let him ask God who will give it to us generously (James 1:5). This particular manifestation in Corinthians is the sudden understanding or revelation from the Holy Spirit concerning a specific problem that you or someone else might be facing. When this gift is manifested, you simply have the insight that leads to a solution. You might be given the understanding for how to accomplish something that you didn't possess before. Bezalel was filled with the Spirit of God, and this experience manifested through wisdom that enabled him to build the tabernacle with great workmanship (Ex. 31:3).

3. Word of Knowledge (*gnosis*)

This knowledge is received from the Holy Spirit to enable us to effectively minister to the needs of people. We suddenly know and understand situations, circumstances, or concerns people might be facing. Sometimes a word of knowledge can be associated with redemption or healing. The first time I witnessed this in my church was a few months after my sabbatical. A man came to me and said he was experiencing a particular pain—and he described it for me. What surprised me, though, was he said that this pain was for someone else. He believed someone was going to be healed from the exact pain that he was experiencing. I was reluctant to share that with the congregation, yet I trusted this person. So I described the exact pain and asked if that related to anyone. Sure enough, someone came forward with the very symptoms that were described. We prayed, and the person was instantly healed. Moreover, the man's pain left his body. We can only describe that as a word of knowledge.

Jesus said the Spirit would even show us things to come (John 16:13). He certainly knew that Judas was going to betray Him (John 13:26). Ananias was given a word of knowledge concerning Paul and what he was going to endure for Jesus' sake (Acts 9:10–16). Paul was filled with the Spirit because Ananias received a word of knowledge. Agabus received a word of knowledge from the Spirit about a famine that prompted the disciples to send relief to the brethren in Judea (Acts 11:28–29). Words of knowledge can be things that we see, sense, dream, or even feel. It is a profound manifestation.

4. Discerning of spirits (*diakresis*)

To discern means to separate through something thoroughly; to distinguish something with accuracy and to know what is correct. This gift is the Spirit-inspired ability to distinguish between good or evil. Paul said that we wrestle against principalities, powers, and rulers in the heavenly realms (Eph. 6:12). When this gift is manifested, it enables someone to pray with boldness because they're able to discern specific strongholds over people, churches, or cities. A person anointed with discernment can sense a spirit of fear or a perverse spirit or a spirit of divination; they're able to accurately discern what spirits could be hindering a person from receiving a touch from God. They are able to test the spirits and see if they are of God (1 John 4:1).

Discernment can sense the move of God's Spirit, too. I have watched people manifest this gift, and they see things that others don't. They are able, with the Spirit's discernment, to gently turn a service into a time when God ministers to the entire church; they don't miss the leading of God because they've accurately discerned God's Spirit. Discernment is a remarkable gift.

Power Manifestations

5. Faith (*pistis*)

Faith is being totally persuaded on a matter. This gift means to have absolute confidence in God and what He has said about an issue. When this gift is manifested, a person suddenly possesses the assurance that God is going to accomplish something significant. It doesn't matter how difficult the circumstances are or what might be a potential hindrance, this person is certain God is going to heal, restore, redeem, or transform an impossible situation. A gift of faith can lift the expectation of an entire church. I have a few people like this in my congregation, and when they step forward and declare, "I've been given faith for this," we know for certain it's only a matter of time before a breakthrough.

A God-given faith led people to do extraordinary things in the Bible. A Roman centurion put his reputation on the line because of faith in Jesus' words (Matt. 8:8–9); two blind men followed Jesus—followed in their blindness—because of faith (Matt. 9:27–28); a woman from Canaan worshipped Jesus after being ignored, insulted, and told it wasn't her hour to receive because she had faith (Matt. 15:21–28); an "unclean" woman pressed through the crowds to touch Jesus because of faith (Mark 5:25–29); four guys ripped through a roof and lowered a make-shift elevator loaded with a crippled man because of faith (Luke 5:18–20); and a sinful woman stood at Jesus' feet, weeping and washing them, because she had faith (Luke 7:37–50). Faith is powerful, to say the least, but when it is activated by the Holy Spirit and manifests as a supernatural gift, extraordinary things will occur.

6. Gifts of healing (*iama*)

The New Testament uses several words to describe "healing." One word is *therapeuo* and from it we derive the English word *therapy*. This word can mean to wait upon, serve, cure, or restore to health. The attitude behind this word therapy is to serve someone as we would serve the Lord. In an attitude of worship and humility unto the Lord, the Spirit will often move upon people bringing restoration physically, emotionally, or spiritually. Jesus often manifested *therapeuo* (see Luke 7:21).

Another word is *kalos* which means to recover or to be made well. This word is used many times in the New Testament, but only once is it used to refer to sick people being restored. In Mark's commission account, Jesus says that one of the signs that will follow those who believe is that they will lay hands on the sick, and they will recover (Mark 16:18).

The word used only in Corinthians (*iama*) means the power to heal, cure, or to bring a remedy. Paul described this particular manifestation as gifts (*charisma*) of healing. The word *gifts* is defined as an anointed endowment or empowerment bestowed on someone, and it is plural which tells us that this empowerment for healing can be displayed in a variety of ways—therapy, recovery, healing, cure, remedy, and so forth. When the Holy Spirit activates healing, it is extraordinary, no matter how it is experienced or through whatever means God chooses. Moreover, there is no set pattern to how healing occurs. Under the inspiration of the Spirit, Jesus spit, declared, and placed His hands on people to execute healing.

I have seen instantaneous healings take place before my eyes, and I have witnessed a slow recovery that took days or weeks. I have witnessed people being healed *from* adversity and I've seen people healed *through* adversity. Healing is a profound gift and a puzzling mystery. I'm certain that the Holy

Spirit will still use people to minister healing. Additionally, as part of our commission, we've all been told to heal the sick (Matt. 10:8; Mark 16:18; Luke 10:9). The gospel of salvation that Paul emphatically stated that he was not ashamed of implies healing and restoration of health physically, emotionally, and spiritually (Rom. 1:16). Healing was part and parcel to the gospel in the New Testament and should be inclusive in our message of salvation, too.

7. Miracles (*dunamis*)

Dunamis is defined as a manifesting influence over reality in a supernatural manner. Miracles are explosive in nature, and they are *supernatural,* meaning that they are beyond human abilities. A few years ago, I watched a woman, who had been bound to a wheelchair for ten years, get out of a wheelchair and walk in front of the altar area of the church—that occurrence was a miracle. That manifestation of power was beyond human capabilities, God delegated the means to enable this woman to walk.

Extraordinary, supernatural manifestations occurred during Jesus' ministry such as raising the dead. Paul experienced unusual miracles during his time in Ephesus (Acts 19:11). Scholars believe that creative miracles took place, such as body parts being replaced or limbs growing back.[125] One of my doctoral cohort members wrote his thesis on metal dissolving from people's bodies, that is, the metal that was surgically implanted due to an injury or for corrective measures. His thesis contains medical documentation to verify the presence and absence of the implanted metal. Another cohort member has seen multiple resurrections from the dead in the particular area of the world where they are ministering. These are modern-day miracles that transpire through the grace and power of the Holy Spirit. We certainly don't chase after them or define our Christian experience by miracles alone, but they are supernatural gifts that God still deploys through His people.

Proclamation Manifestations

8. Tongues (*glossa*)

This word simply means language or inspired speech. When this gift is manifested, it usually means that someone is articulating a message in ways not originated by human skills or effort. No other gift in the list of nine has caused as much grief and division as this one. It was a problem for the Corinthian believers and probably is what prompted Paul to begin his discussion of the *charismata* by addressing their ignorance (1 Cor. 12:1).

Paul identified this gift by stating "kinds" (*genos*) of tongues. This word *genos* carries the meaning of species, family, assortment, or variety. This word "kinds" tells us that the gift of tongues may not be displayed as only *one* manifestation; there may be a variety of ways this particular gift is manifested. The Bible identifies four varieties of tongues in the New Testament. They are as follows: other tongues (Acts 2:4), angelic tongues (1 Cor. 13:1), prayer/worship tongues (1 Cor. 14:14), and new tongues (Mark 16:17). Let's briefly examine each of these.

First, there are different tongues evident in Acts, "they began to speak with other tongues" (Acts 2:4). The word "other" is *heteros,* and means something similar; it's different in style or form. In the context of Acts during Pentecost, there were devout men gathered from every nation. During the outpouring of the Holy Spirit, all of these devout men from eighteen different nations heard the upper room believers speaking the mighty works of God in their own language (*dialektos*) or in their own dialects (Acts 2:8). Most scholarly evidence points to the fact that the inspired disciples were speaking *unlearned* languages (human dialects) under the unction of the Holy Spirit. The same thought is attributed to the other two references to tongues in Acts (Acts 10:44–46; 19:6).

Second, we have angelic tongues (1 Cor. 13:1). We know the least about angelic tongues, but most expositors describe these tongues as heavenly, celestial language. Paul used this description as a bit of hyperbole stating that angelic tongues, or any other gift for that matter, does not surpass love—love does not fail (1 Cor. 13:8). Angelic tongues can also be messages given to mankind usually communicated through dreams or visions; such is the case with Peter (Acts 10:3, 10).

Third, we have what is known as a private prayer/worship tongues. I use the word private because Paul said, "He who speaks in a tongue does not speak to men but to God" (1 Cor. 14:2). Donald Metz, writing for the Church of the Nazarene said, "The man exercising this gift is not speaking unto men but is involved in a personal expression of praise to God."[126] Metz was not *authorizing* the (public) use of this expression for Nazarenes, but he was *legitimizing* the gift. It is a recognizable expression of the Holy Spirit used in certain applications: namely, in private with God. This is a heavenly language known only to God. Metz went on to say that this gift should not be forbidden or despised, for it may have value when used in a proper time and place.[127]

Dick Howard, former professor of New Testament and Greek at Bethany Nazarene College, now Southern Nazarene University, described this particular gift as a "spirit language" meaning this is a language sourced by the Holy Spirit. Howard spoke to the point that the deepest part of our lives is our spirit, and praying in tongues is the Holy Spirit praying through us in worship or adoration from that deep part of our lives.[128] That is why Paul said, "If I pray in a tongue, my spirit prays" (1 Cor. 14:14). But while this type of Spirit-manifested prayer may edify the believer's spirit (1 Cor. 14:4), it transcends the mind, so Paul was quick to say we should pray for interpretation if we desire to be enlightened in the mind (1 Cor. 14:13–14).

Paul did not encourage the public display of this gift. Tongues are not to be forbidden, though (1 Cor. 14:39), so a companion gift of interpretation is to accompany the public manifestation of tongues. However, the instructions given for the interpretation of tongues in the assembly (1 Cor. 14:27–28) were not given so the Corinthian congregation *would* speak in tongues publically, but *if* they continued. In other words, Paul was not instructing them how to speak in tongues in the assembly as much as giving correction to a problem that seemed to persist. In short, prophecy should be the public manifestation, and prayer/worship tongues should be the private manifestation.

Fourth, Jesus talked about new tongues (Mark 16:17). New tongues are not unknown tongues, but anointed tongues; it is speech that is evidenced with a new unction and power. It is language that is prompted and anointed by the Holy Spirit as a result of the redemptive work of Jesus Christ. This type of tongue is described by Jesus as "new" (*kainos*), a word that describes something that has been made new in terms of substance or form; something that has been regenerated. The Bible identifies twelve specific things that have been made new as a result of the regenerating power of Christ. They are as follows: new wine (Matt. 9:17), New Covenant (Matt. 26:28), new commandment (John 13:34), new creation (2 Cor. 5:17), new creature (Gal. 6:16), new man (Eph. 2:15), new name (Rev. 2:17), new song (Rev. 5:9), new heaven (Rev. 21:1), new earth (Rev. 21:1), new Jerusalem (Rev. 21:2), and our passage in Mark 16:17 where Jesus refers to new tongues.

Peter demonstrated new tongues on the day of Pentecost when he stood up and spoke to the crowds. In Acts 1:15, Peter stood and "said" something to the people in the upper room. This word simply means that he spoke—no big deal, but in Acts 2:14, the word *said* has a different meaning. In this passage, it means to utter or speak under the influence of the Spirit. It is the same word used in Acts 2:4 when it says that the disciples spoke as the Spirit "gave them utterance." Years ago, people like E. M. Bounds and Leonard Ravenhill talked about preaching with "unction." They meant speaking with the power of the Spirit. When Peter finished speaking in "new tongues" three thousand people were "cut" to the heart and moved to respond (Acts 2:37). I believe that Peter spoke with unction; he spoke with the power of the Spirit.

While I don't want to suggest that we have to speak in any variety of tongues, I will tell you that new tongues are a sign of believing and following Jesus. "These signs will follow," Jesus said (Mark 16:17). We'll expand upon this more in the next chapter, but when we've been with Jesus and empowered by His presence, we are going to speak differently. Peter and John, two uneducated and untrained disciples, made the leaders of Israel marvel because of their boldness of speech (Acts 4:13). I believe that they spoke with a new language; a language anointed with the power of the Spirit. We desperately need men and women to speak *only* as the Spirit gives them utterance. We need to hear a *new* language—language seasoned with salt (Col. 4:6) and language that imparts grace (Eph. 4:19). Jesus' words were filled with life (John 6:63); should we expect anything less—should we settle for less? Doesn't a lost and dying world need all of our prayers, speaking, preaching, and teaching to be spoken with unction and power that gives evidence that we've been in Jesus?

9. Interpretation of Tongues (*hermeneia*)

To interpret something means to translate a message and clearly explain what has been communicated. When this gift is manifested, it allows the body of Christ to be edified, exhorted, or comforted by a message that has been spoken through a tongue. Keep in mind that while tongues are varied, so is the gift of interpretation. Sometimes God speaks through dreams and visions, so a person manifesting this gift can interpret those messages and give meaning to the assembly. Other people manifesting this gift have the anointed ability to sense God's messages in moments of great difficulty and can instill hope, faith, and clarity to otherwise adverse situations in people's lives.

Doers of the Word: A Supernatural Lifestyle

Somewhere along the line the Jewish believers in the book of James had to experience a discipleship lesson or two. At least we know that they were "hearers" of the Word, which is a good place to start for any pupil. But James realized that greater blessings come by putting the Word into action—blessed in what he does (1:25). So James told these believers to become "doers" of what they hear (1:22). This word "doers" (*poietes*) has been described as someone who performs or acts upon a script. We might think of a playwright who has written a script for his performers. He expects the actors to perform the script that has been written for them.

Another way to look at this is that Jesus said that if we love Him, we will obey His commandments (John 14:15). Commandments are "prescriptions" that have been given to us. Jesus is the One who writes the script; we are to obey every word He says. We are to perform or to put into action His *pre*script—the script that He's prepared in advance for us. This is what being a doer of the Word is about. It's obeying Jesus' commands; activating His script.

It's amazing what can happen when we actually put His word into action. According to James, a doer of the Word will care for orphans and widows, activate faith, conduct their lives in meekness, submit to God, live in humility, speak no evil of the brethren, live with patience, and that is just getting started. The pragmatic lifestyle that James outlined was accompanied by supernatural results, too. He said, "The prayer of faith will save the sick, and the Lord will raise him up. And if he has committed sins, he will be forgiven" (5:15). To save (*sozo*) the sick is nothing short of supernatural transformation; saving the sick is restoration of the body, mind, and spirit. James said an atmosphere is created where God can "raise people up," a possible reference to raising the dead. Moreover, in this anointed atmosphere of being doers of His Word, sins will be forgiven, and prayers will be powerful and effective like the days of Elijah (5:16–18). James described a supernatural culture, not a program or a classroom discipleship lesson. When we activate the Word of God, we start to develop a supernatural lifestyle that goes beyond the classroom and church walls. James was describing a lifestyle of the Word and the Spirit in action.

I recently had the privilege to participate in a large prayer gathering in Kansas City organized by Dan and Carol Ketchum, well known, loved, and respected by many in the Church of the Nazarene. One particular afternoon, the presence of God was heavy upon us. There were people praying, worshipping, and ministering in every part of the room. I saw people receive instant healing, deliverance from sin, restored hope and vision, and one person even experienced freedom from demonic oppression. It was like being in the river of God as described in Ezekiel 47; it was refreshing and totally free of religious paradigms, and yet there was nothing out of order or divisive. It was a room filled with God's people being doers of the Word under the leadership and guidance of the Holy Spirit. The supernatural gifts were being deployed through God's instruments with decency and order, and those gathered were edified and blessed as a result of His Spirit manifesting through each of us.

There is nothing superficial or phony about a supernatural lifestyle that I just described. I realize that there is a great concern among many in non-Pentecostal Holiness churches that somehow we're being influenced by a new (neo) Pentecostal wave. Yet when I read the accounts of early Nazarenes and Methodists, I wonder if we've drifted so far from our heritage that we don't remember what we looked like. C. B. Jernigan, a former district superintendent in the Church of the Nazarene, wrote a book entitled, *Pioneer Days of the Holiness Movement in the Southwest*. His book chronicles the events in the late 1800s leading up to the formation of the Church of the Nazarene. He writes of people being instantly born again, sanctified, falling to the ground (sometimes for days) under the power of God, healed and delivered; meetings would extend for days, and the conviction of God upon people would cause them to scream aloud, run to the altar, shake, or fall prostrate in the dirt.

Reading Jernigan's book revealed three consistent characteristics with these Christians. First, they were relentless in their preaching of holiness. In spite of ridicule and persecution, their message never changed: sanctification, purity, and deeper cleansing. Second, they functioned with extraordinary power, and that power was recognized by believers and nonbelievers alike. Like the early church, "fear came upon every soul" (Acts 2:43) of those who were around these Christians because people realized that they were possessed with an awesome power. Third, they were desperate for God, and that desperation never waned. Their hunger for God made them willing to sacrifice time, money, and resources for greater encounters with Him. Most of all, these early Christians referenced by Jernigan lived a supernatural lifestyle; these believers of the 1800s, who were the foundation of the Holiness movement, were doers of the Word. They experienced the supernatural because they lived the Word. Jernigan said, "These were like the days of the Acts of the Apostles, and if people would go whole souled into the Word of the Lord today as then they would see the same results."[129]

There's a popular teaching today that warns believers about "strange fire" in our churches. The teaching taken from Leviticus 10 attacks the charismatic gifts and the lifestyle described in this chapter. I can assure you that I'm not advocating a lifestyle of mindless ecstasy and spiritual abuses. We have all witnessed unbiblical practices and carnal manifestations in the body of Christ. But honestly, spiritual excess does not concern me as much as spiritual lack. I'm most concerned when the lifestyle commissioned by Jesus and demonstrated by His followers is questioned within mainstream evangelicalism as "unneeded activities" for the Church. To dumb down the supernatural activities of the Bible in fear of "strange fire" or sensationalism is no less than alarming. I don't fear "strange fire" in the Church as much as I fear "no fire." Where are the gifts? Where are the supernatural works? Where are the miracles? Well, "we don't chase after them" is the comment that I hear. I agree with that statement, but we've chased them off! The problem with too many churches in America is that the fire has been quenched, a violation spoken about in 1 Thessalonians 5:19. We *need* the fire; we *need* the Holy Spirit, and we must have the fervency of the Spirit that Paul spoke about (Rom. 12:11).

My heart breaks as I travel and sit through church services that are cold and dead. There are too many people who lack spiritual hunger, too many believers who are weary and burned-out, too many Christians who are numb and bored, and too many church goers who know doctrines and creeds of their particular church or denomination, but they possess no zeal or hope that their cities or even their own spiritual life can be transformed by God. There are too many Christians today who are not passionate for the things of God. They don't pray with expectancy or worship with intensity. They don't come before God with an expectation of encountering His manifest presence. So when I hear that people are cautious and skeptical about living in the supernatural or question

129

the spiritual gifts as valid manifestations for today, my heart is grieved. We really *do* have a problem in the Holiness movement. It is time to wake up! The Holiness movement needs to *move* again. Churches of every denomination need to respond to the commission (prescription) given to us by Jesus. The Holy Spirit is longing to quicken our hearts for, among other things, a fresh impartation of the gifts so that we can flow like a river into the deepest valleys and bring healing, restoration, redemption, and revival to our land. So how must we posture ourselves in order to sustain a supernatural lifestyle? Let's learn about the life that is in the voice.

Chapter Nine

Life Is in the Voice

—◦◦◦—

J esus was teaching one day when His message was inter-
rupted by someone who apparently was overcome by feel-
ings of motherhood. A woman screamed aloud in the middle
of His message, "Blessed is the womb that bore You, and
the breasts which nursed you" (Luke 11:27). Okay, I'm not
sure how I would have responded to that comment. I've had
many unusual events occur while I've been preaching, but I
would be hard pressed to think of anything that could top that.
Jesus didn't rebuke this woman; instead He redirected the
blessing by saying, "More than that, blessed are those who
hear the word of God and keep it" (Luke 11:28). The word
"keep" (*phulasso*) comes from a root word that actually means
to produce, germinate, or grow something. The best way to
guard or keep God's Word is to put it into productivity. So
we are back to being a doer of the Word. In Jesus' response,
there is a phrase that I want to emphasize, and I believe it
holds the key to replicating His lifestyle. In order to produce
or activate the Word of God we must "hear the Word." If we
could shorten the phrase that Jesus spoke to this woman, I
would state it this way: "Blessings on those who hear." Life is
in His voice, so we must be close enough to hear Him speak.

I love the scene where Jesus came into Bethany, and He entered a certain woman's house whose name was Martha. She had a sister called Mary. We have no idea how long Jesus was at this house, but the Bible is clear concerning the mindset of both women. Mary "sat" at Jesus' feet and heard His Word (Luke 10:39). This word "sat" (*parakathidzo*) is only used here in the New Testament, and it is used by someone who was particular with details. The author Luke, a physician by trade, was attempting, I believe, to set up a contrast between Mary and Martha. Mary sat at Jesus' feet, which literally means to sit against Him. The word that Luke chose describes proximity; it tells us that Mary pressed in. It describes someone who is spiritually hungry; they can't wait to hear what is spoken, and as a result they get as close as they can to hear every single word. Being at the feet of a rabbi in the first century demonstrated a posture of humility and receptivity to instruction. Nothing else seemed to matter to Mary during those moments, and she did the one thing that was most needed according to Jesus.

How would your life look if you postured yourself before Jesus every day to hear His words? I'm not simply talking about having your quiet time with the Lord, but I'm talking about developing a lifestyle that is lived out of intimacy. Jesus pressed in to the Father. He was so close to the Father that His ears were against the chest—in the bosom of the Father (John 1:18). Jesus lived on what the Father said; He lived with the presence of the Spirit upon Him every moment (John 1:32). Jesus reminded us that whatever He spoke, no matter what He said, it was exactly what the Father said (John 12:50). Jesus demonstrated a lifestyle of intimacy; He only said what the Father said, and He only did what the Father did. Jesus was so close to the Father—so intimate—that He said if you see Him, you see the Father (John 14:9). Can that statement be said about us? Can people look at us and see the presence of the Father? I want to be so close to Jesus that when I open my mouth, His words spring forth; when people are around me, they'll know I'm a child of God because they'll see the resemblance.

There is an ocean between being a servant of Jesus and a friend of His. Jesus said that servants don't know what the master is doing (John 15:15). Their obedience is out of duty, and they lack an intimate relationship with the master that would warrant more information than "go here" or "do that." Jesus describes us as friends, and friends serve out of love; friendship implies intimacy, and friends are made aware of what the Father is doing. Jesus said, "It has been given to you to know the mysteries of the kingdom of heaven" in Matthew 13:11, and He said in verse 16, "Blessed are our ears" because of what we are privileged to hear. What a blessing given to each of us! We can hear His voice, and life is in that voice.

Mary chose to sit at Jesus' feet and hear His Word in this account in Luke 10, but what about her sister, Martha? Some of the most sobering words describe the mindset of Martha, the Bible says she was "distracted" (Luke 10:40). Luke used one word to describe Mary's position—she "sat" in His presence, and he used one word to describe Martha's position—she was "distracted." Distraction (*perispao*) is a word that means to drag around, to be driven in circles, or to draw away. Jesus dispensed words of life; when Jesus spoke, tremendous things happened: disease was cured, demons fled, water transformed, storms ceased, ears opened, eyes saw, mouths spoke, and best of all, the poor had the gospel preached to them. Great things happened when Jesus spoke words. Why, because life is in His voice (John 6:63). Mary heard those words spoken by Jesus because she chose to be pressed against His feet while Martha was driven and dragged around in circles; in fact, she remained distracted even in His presence. I realize that she was remarkable woman, and her faith in Jesus was demonstrated in John 11, but on this occasion Martha was worried and troubled about many things.

Her mind was not at rest; she was provoked and anxious, and therefore, she didn't benefit from the life-changing words given by Jesus.

When Ministry Becomes a Distraction

Why was Martha being dragged around in circles to begin with? Here's the real heartbreak in this story, she was distracted with much *serving*. Her ministry became the very thing that preoccupied her, causing her to lose the voice. This passage implies that she was doing ministry without actually intently listening to Jesus' words. How does that work? How do we become doers of the Word if we aren't hearing the Word?

Like Martha, we will make spiritual assumptions when we're not actually hearing Him. As far as we can discern from this text, Martha was not asked to make preparations for Jesus. In fact, when Jesus rebuked Martha, He was underscoring Mary's activity—sitting at His feet, while at the same time correcting Martha on her poor choice. The ministry that Martha chose to do on that particular occasion was self-induced. Martha might have wanted to serve with the right intentions, but she was anxious, troubled, and distressed about many things. She was not living or ministering out of the voice in this particular scene.

Distraction can be a real issue for all of us, not just for those who are in full-time ministry, but for anyone desiring to minister. How can we replicate Jesus if we're distracted from His presence? How do we operate in the power of His presence if we're running in circles? How can we function in the supernatural if we're overwhelmed by the natural? We must realize that a Word-and-Spirit life will not be possible unless we're positioned in such a way to hear His voice. When ministry becomes a distraction, terrible things start to happen:

- We will make *good* decisions, but not *God* decisions;
- We will be filled with *activities,* but not *accomplishments*;
- We will get *weary,* but fail to *worship*;
- We will see *problems,* but fail to see the *possibilities*;
- We will become *burned-out,* but not be *fired-up*;
- We will do things *for* Jesus, but not *from* Him; and
- We will cease being *prophetic,* and merely become *pathetic*.

When ministry becomes a distraction, we have ceased serving from a posture of intimacy that's focused on Jesus; rather, we have exchanged our *posture* with Christ for a *position* in ministry. The focus is no longer being with Him, but fulfilling our task for Him. Even while we might be doing good things for God, the church, or even in the community, our activities will lack the power of the supernatural. We will find ourselves simply running in circles and accomplishing very little for the kingdom of God.

There's a very interesting conjunction in Luke 10:39. The verse reads, "And she had a sister called Mary who *also* sat at Jesus' feet and heard His Word [emphasis mine]." The only reason that conjunction is there is because Luke was trying to tell us something about Martha. She occupied the same position Mary was in at least one time in her life. However, this time Martha was not doing what she once did before. Why? No one really knows the answer to that question. But what we do know is that Martha had experienced a shift in her focus. Like Peter, she had taken her eyes off Jesus and looked at the wind and the waves. She was filled with anxiety and many concerns, and it robbed her from the voice. Worse still, she made a spiritual assumption that ministry was to be preferred over hearing Jesus' words. Truth be told, she represents many of us in the Church today who have worked hard, persevered, labored, and ministered with great patience, but we have left our first love (Rev. 2:4). We're no longer at His feet listening to His Word; we're missing the *one* thing that matters most. We may have started out hearing His voice, but time, perhaps even ministry, has overshadowed hearing the life-changing words of Jesus.

The Perils of Distraction

The story of Martha and Mary has been a source of revelation for me, while at the same time, it has been troubling for me. Martha's actions are the most disturbing aspect of this encounter. She approached Jesus and said, "Lord, do you not care that my sister has left me to serve alone? Therefore tell her to help me" (Luke 10:40). Her question to Jesus was a rebuke, and then she essentially demanded that Jesus stop His ministry so Mary could fulfill her ministry. In other words, "Hey Jesus, I know you're dispensing truths that are life-changing, but could You stop so Mary could help me in the kitchen?" People who are distracted will distract others. If you have someone on the team who isn't close enough to hear Jesus' voice, they will become the instrument that will disturb others from hearing Him.

There are many lessons learned when you are in the ministry. Over the years, I've learned that the most productive and effective leader or staff member that I can have on the team is someone who lives in intimacy with Jesus. This lesson, to me, is more important than their skills or abilities because if they are well-schooled in the school of the Spirit through a life of intimacy with Christ, the Holy Spirit will instruct them, empower them, and equip them for any ministry assignments. If someone comes to the table preoccupied, however, and they're making spiritual assumptions, it won't be long until our plans will deviate off course. Even worse, when distracted people lead a ministry, and they haven't chosen the good part like Mary did in Luke 10, they will inevitably lead people away from His presence. Distracted people will place more emphasis on their project or ministry, and the more overwhelmed and disheveled they feel, the more they'll cajole people into their plans. Martha's ministry was so significant in her eyes that she demanded Jesus to stop teaching so her ministry could prevail over His.

Another concern that I have with distracted people is that they will make decisions based on the wrong premises. For example, in Mark 1, Jesus was ministering in Capernaum, and He entered the synagogue on the Sabbath to teach. While He was teaching, a man with an unclean spirit experienced deliverance. With a few words, Jesus cast the spirit out, and all the people were amazed. Immediately after the service was over, Jesus' fame spreads all over the region of Galilee to the point that by the end of the day, people were lined up for ministry. That evening Jesus healed all who were sick; He cast out demons and delivered people from various diseases. The Bible tells us that the whole city experienced the blessing of this one-night crusade.

We have no idea how late into the night this ministry event lasted, but early the next morning, Jesus got up before anyone else and went to a solitary place to pray. In light of the victories of the day before, Jesus consciously chose to "get to the feet" of His Father. After some time passed, the disciples eventually found Jesus and explained to Him that everyone was looking for Him. In other words, they were ready for day two of this ministry crusade. And why not think that? In view of what occurred the day before, if I was a disciple of Jesus I would have thought no different. I would have had Jesus' ministry table and CDs set up and the band fully rehearsed, and I would have been ready for an even greater service than the night before!

The tendency for distracted people is to make decisions based on results. If something is successful, we reason, why not do it again? It must be God's will or we wouldn't have had such a great turnout. I have watched many "successful ministry events" turn cold and become a mere performance of the flesh because the Spirit was no longer leading the event. Distracted people will miss the subtle voice of Jesus and will put their allegiance into their ministry task. No matter how good your intentions are, if you are making a ministry assumption—like Martha did—you will disturb others from being in His presence, and you'll miss His voice yourself. Jesus, after praying early that morning, said to His disciples, "Let us go" (Mark 1:38). He shut the crusade down after just one night and went elsewhere to preach before He came back to Capernaum at a later date. Why did Jesus do that? The answer is because life is in the voice. He heard the voice of the Father and obeyed. Just like Jesus, we must base all decisions on His presence and not on our programs.

I've read many books about ministry burnout, and I believe it is an unfortunate tragedy. Burnout nearly ruined my life and ministry, so I believe in the necessity of these books and resources. But as I sorted through the debris in my life that led me to burnout, I realized that the culprit was living life without hearing the voice. Have I told you lately that life is in the voice? I'm really serious about that statement. Jesus says we don't live by bread alone, but we *do* live by every single word that proceeds out of God's mouth (Matt. 4:4). Jesus was quoting an Old Testament passage in Deuteronomy 8:3, where God fed His people with a "mystery" bread called manna. God actually humbled the people by allowing them to feel hunger, and then He fed them with something from heaven. The real miracle in this story is not the manna, but the utterance of God. There is no word in this passage to describe what comes out of God's mouth. So when Jesus quotes this passage in Deuteronomy referring to what proceeds out of God's mouth, He used the word *rhema*, which means something uttered that is living: a living voice or a voice filled with life. Every word that Jesus speaks is filled with life; anything uttered out of God's mouth is something that we can live on. Words spoken out of heaven contain nutrients from another world called the kingdom of God. These words are not "fast food" or empty calories, but they are nutrient-dense, anointed, life-giving morsels that change destinies, heal bodies, deliver the oppressed, and bring people into encounters with the living God. The words from Jesus' mouth are supernatural.

If we aren't hearing supernatural words, we're limited to mere "natural" words; words originating from this realm, words that contain the nature of flesh. If we live by every word that proceeds out of God's mouth, then we die in their absence. I was near spiritual death prior to my sabbatical because much of my ministry had been built on good ideas and not God ideas. Like Martha, I was running in circles. Sadly, my congregation reflected my life, and they were spiritually stagnant and lifeless. No one was having encounters with God: we didn't see any miracles, people weren't being transformed or delivered from demonic oppression, bodies weren't being healed, and believers weren't being sanctified. Yes, the mercy and grace of God did things in people that I may never see this side of eternity, and I realize that by the foolishness of preaching, God accomplished things in spite of me. Yet for most of my ministry, I was missing the voice. Minister with the mindset of Martha for very long, and you will burn out.

To this mix was added a steady diet of church-growth books that were being hyped as the answer to every church dilemma. These resources outlined every possible technique to make my church relevant and appealing. Being young and impressionable, I consumed them all with the voracious, insatiable appetite of a fifteen-year-old boy. Even my criteria to evaluate pastoral success were locked into a system of ecclesiastical procedures that year after year examined statistics. So I felt compelled to produce and even guilty if I didn't reveal results that had little to do with actual New Testament standards.

What is even more detrimental is to think that some of our academic environments may supplant their voice for the voice of God. The story in 1 Kings 13 entails an unsettling account of a young prophet who heard the voice of the Lord but became distracted. He entered a city to cry against it for defiling the altar, something that he was commissioned to do, rather than the older prophet who lived in that particular area. The young prophet was adamant about obeying the Word of the Lord—he heard the voice, and he wasn't going to deviate from his mission. After the young prophet displayed super-natural power, the king invited him to dinner but to no avail. The young prophet was not enticed by prestige. Besides, he told the king that he must obey God's voice—the Word of the Lord. All seemed well until the older prophet of the city invited the younger prophet over to have a meal with him. The younger prophet responded with the same defense: he must obey the Word of the Lord. But there's an interesting twist in this story. The older prophet lied and told the younger prophet that he too had heard a "word" from the Lord. The younger prophet relented, and the "rest of the story" is tragic, indeed, because he was killed by a lion.

How is this account any different, asked Ruthven, for God-called ministers seeking training from prestigious, accredited seminaries that, instead of confirming their faith and helping them remain sensitive to His voice, like the voice of the older prophet, "often mislead and stretch their students' faith beyond the breaking point."[130] Our Christian schools have a tremendous responsibility to equip students, but they cannot, in the arrogance of academia, become a superior voice to the simple guidance of the Holy Spirit. To be honest, looking back to my college and seminary training, I can't recall too many experiences that helped or taught me to listen to the voice of God. It was assumed that ministry students prayed, recognized, and listened to the voice of the Holy Spirit. As a result, we busied ourselves to learn *other* things. I'm not suggesting that core requirements be abolished, but I would suggest incorporating lessons that help students learn to listen and activate the voice of the Holy Spirit. Additionally, colleges and seminaries need to be very careful that they don't squelch the faith of vulnerable students. While I had some professors who taught me to appreciate the Bible and to value the leadership of the Holy Spirit, I also experienced a few who made me question the basic principles of faith or whether I *could* hear God's voice. The end result for any of us who bypass God's voice is the same; it may not be a lion that kills us, but we will be just as dead.[131]

The Bible says that when Adam heard the voice of God in the garden, he ran and hid because he was naked (Gen. 3:10). Adam had been stripped of his relationship with God because he gave way to another voice. God's voice brought fear, not peace, because Adam became attached to an earthly voice. In Genesis 3:17, the Bible says that Adam listened to the voice of his wife. Eve's voice triumphed over God's voice; Adam was seduced by a voice of reason, and he accepted that voice as a superior truth to the words spoken by God. Death entered the human race because of Adam's sin. Spiritual death always follows those who allow human reasoning, circumstances, experiences, education, or anything for that matter, to speak louder than the voice of God. This lesson is so simple that we often miss it. Our entire living experience and all of our ministry endeavors must be established on the voice of the Lord. Life is in His voice.

Ministry out of Intimacy

Isaiah 55:3 says, "Incline your ear and come to Me. Hear, and your soul shall live." To incline your ear means to lean in, to bend toward something. In this verse, Isaiah was challenging us to lean into the Lord so that we could hear Him speak. The benefit of hearing, Isaiah said, is that our soul will live. Spiritual life and vitality are only found in His voice, so we are to bend toward Him to hear His words. Later in the same chapter, Isaiah explained that the Word of the Lord is effective when it is dispatched (v. 11). The writer of Hebrews said, "For the Word of God is living and powerful" (Heb. 4:12). Something always happens when we hear and speak His words. His Word will never return void. If God's words are powerful and effective, and His words always accomplish their intended purpose, then it is essential that we develop the kind of lifestyle where we are ministering from a position of intimacy with Christ.

In John 12:3, we see Mary on another occasion taking costly oil and anointing the feet of Jesus, an act of ministry that the distracted disciple failed to do. Because Mary had sat at Jesus' feet and listened to His Word, she was equipped to minister in a profound manner. In fact, because the disciples were so preoccupied with other things (voices), they became indignant with Mary's outrageous display of worship (Matt. 26:8). Jesus' statement to Mary must be underscored. He told her that "wherever the gospel is preached in the whole world," her act of ministry will be told as well (Matt. 26:13). Mary's ministry was significant. She learned something at the feet of Jesus in Luke 10:39 that Martha and the disciples failed to see; she heard something in her position of intimacy that enabled her to fulfill a single act of ministry that will have global recognition. I can't think of too many things that I've done so far that will have a global impact. I'm not looking for recognition, but I do want to minister out of a position of intimacy because then whatever I do will produce fruit that lasts.

Another consideration is that when Mary poured the spikenard oil over the feet of Jesus, the fragrance filled the house. Mary's position of intimacy culminated in releasing a fragrance that permeated the room; Mary and Jesus smelled identical, and their intimate relationship affected others around them. The atmosphere of the room was changed because of this woman's ministry. If we develop a life of intimacy with Christ, we will affect the atmosphere wherever we go. Paul said we are to be the fragrance of Christ (2 Cor. 2:15). If we've been in His presence, we will smell like Him; we'll start to release His fragrance in our world. That means when we walk into an environment, having been immersed in His presence, our lives are going to diffuse His nature. We have the possibility to affect cities and cultures; we can release His presence amidst "stinking" messes.

Let's examine this idea from another perspective. Jesus said, "Go into all the world and preach the gospel to every creature" (Mark 16:15). The word "preach" (*kerusso*) is a verb that means to proclaim, to speak, to declare, or to herald a message. It is derived from the noun *kerux*.[132] A *kerux* was a spokesman, who had a special assignment from the king. Their function was twofold. First, they were to enter the chamber room of the king and listen to every word spoken. A *kerux* listened to the tone, meaning, emotion, and intent of the word. Second, when they left the presence of the king, they spoke to the people on behalf of the king. They spoke exactly what the king said, and did so in the manner, emotions, and intent of the king. So their assignment was to listen and speak. That assignment sounds familiar, doesn't it? Our assignment is the same. We are to enter the chamber room of our King, a place of intimacy, listen to His words, spend time with Him, learn from Him, and then we go into the world and speak what He has said.

The disciples knew exactly what Jesus was describing when He told them to preach the gospel. He was calling them to a life of intimacy. The assignment, and the empowerment, to announce the good news was contingent upon being in the presence of the King. Preaching the gospel is only effective if we've emerged out of the chamber room with God, our

King, and we are releasing His words, His way. Perhaps the reason the gospel has not transformed the American culture is because the church is too busy to sit before the King. If you think about it, the gospel is being propagated by every form of media such as: TV, radio, Internet, smart phones, you name it; we're covered with the gospel. Yet, America is becoming less Christian. The preaching of the gospel doesn't seem to be making a widespread difference in the United States. Perhaps the reason for the lack of power in our messages is because we know little about intimacy with our King in His chamber room. Isaiah cried out, "Come, my people, enter your chambers" (Isa. 26:20). The Psalmist talked about dwelling in the secret place of the Most High (Ps. 91:1). It is only when we've been with the Most High in His chambers will our message have any impact. Jesus called His disciples to a ministry that reflected a lifestyle of intimacy with the Lord.

What would it look like to be a *kerux* in light of the New Covenant? Our hearts become the chamber room for the King's presence through the infilling of the Holy Spirit. So in reality, we can live in intimacy with the King of all kings and hear Him speak moment by moment. We actually can say what He is "saying" because He speaks to us through His Spirit. When I describe the life of Mary in Luke 10, I'm not advocating that we merely sit around and listen to Jesus speak. Although times of solitude with the Lord are vital to maintain a vibrant Christian life, I'm talking about developing a lifestyle of living out of His voice. I believe it's not only possible but imperative to live with our hearts in communion with the Holy Spirit all day long. We might be busy externally, yet be at rest and postured in His presence in our hearts. We never have to leave His presence! We can "sit at His feet" in our hearts and fulfill the ever-demanding responsibilities that we have. Every moment of our lives can be immersed by His presence, and nothing around us needs to become larger in our minds than His manifest presence that is with us—and within us. I'm describing a lifestyle of walking in the Spirit. Jesus told us that the Spirit would dwell with us and would be in us (John 14:17).

What happens when we minister out of intimacy? What happens when we minister in and through the presence of the Spirit? We become doers of the Word. Our lifestyles start to personify the supernatural presence of the Holy Spirit with whom we're dwelling every moment of each day. Mark described this lifestyle when he wrote, "And they went out and preached everywhere, the Lord working with them and confirming the word through the accompanying signs" (Mark 16:20). The disciples' message had power attached to it; they preached the Word, and it was accompanied with signs because they worked in congruency with the Lord. Many scholars attach this verse to post-Pentecost, so it's describing the abiding presence of the Holy Spirit empowering the disciples.

What Jesus described is possible for all Christians, not just the early believers. In fact, Jesus said four signs will follow those who believe (Mark 16:17). Keep in mind the context of what we've discussed so far. To believe is to dwell in His presence as a *kerux;* it is to be filled with the Spirit and walk in the Spirit. Believing implies an intimate, ongoing relationship with Jesus through the Holy Spirit. Jesus was describing ministry out of intimacy in Mark 16. The four signs that Jesus identified are the following: extrication, communication, preservation, and restoration.

First, Jesus said, "In My name they will cast out demons" (Mark 16:17). This is the sign of extrication. We don't look for demons; I'm not advocating demon hunting by any means. In fact, I'm cautious around people who seem to talk more about the devil than Jesus. But one of the signs that follows a *kerux* is they will cast out demons. Our lives should be so filled with the Spirit, so immersed with Christ's scent, so anointed with His presence, that demons have a hard time remaining in or on someone who we're ministering to. I remember a counseling situation where the Holy Spirit impressed upon me a specific question to ask of this person. When I did, the person fell to the floor, on their hands and knees, like a dog and started growling at me. For a brief moment, I panicked and thought to myself, "What am I going to do? I'm not equipped to deal with this; how do I handle this?" Then I realized that I was positioned in intimacy with Jesus; I was resting in His presence. So in Jesus' name, I spoke freedom over this person, and after a few minutes, the person was set free from that demonic manifestation. Jesus modeled this as He went about healing all who were oppressed by the devil (Acts 10:38). If we're intimate with Him, His activities will eventually become our activities. One of those signs will be extrication.

Second, Jesus mentioned the sign of communication. He said "they will speak in new tongues" (Mark 16:17). We discussed this in the last chapter, but just a quick reminder: This is not an unknown tongue, rather an anointed tongue. In the context, Jesus was talking about preaching the gospel. When we, as a *kerux,* have been in His presence, and continue to walk in His presence through the Holy Spirit, our words are going to be anointed with the Spirit. Our language will be sourced by a power that is *super*natural. Our communication will be fresh, inspiring, and fragrant; it will give evidence of the One we're intimate with. Paul said, "Let no corrupt word proceed out of your mouths, but what is good and necessary edification, that it may impart grace to the hearers" (Eph. 4:29). What is a corrupt word? A corrupt word is lifeless; it's a word spoken that is sourced by our flesh, it's rotten and fruitless. Now insert a Christian (*kerux*) who is walking in the Spirit; when they start speaking they edify the listener. In fact, they impart grace (*charis*), which is a supernatural force. Our language should give us away. The way you talk gives evidence of what you're filled with. Jesus said, "For out of the abundance of the heart the mouth speaks" (Matt. 12:34). You will talk either with "old tongues" (language sourced by flesh) or with new tongues. If you live in intimacy with the King, and walk in the Spirit, your communication will be new.

The third sign that Jesus mentioned is preservation. He said, "They will take up serpents; and if they drink anything deadly, it will by no means hurt them" (Mark 16:18). Images and stories instantly fill my mind of accounts of some foolish behavior over this verse! Once again, keep this verse in the context. Someone who is walking in the Spirit and intimate with God will not die before their appointed time, so they can rest through any adversity—they will be preserved. Jesus demonstrated this point in Mark 4 when He slept during a great windstorm that threatened to sink the boat. He told His disciples to cross over to the other side. Remember that Jesus only said what His Father said, so Jesus spoke out of intimacy. The Father gave Jesus His commission, so Jesus could rest in that assignment—no matter what. He rested because He knew He was not going to die; Jesus demonstrated the sign of preservation.

Paul was given a word from the Lord that he must be brought before Caesar; Paul rested in that word. He walked in the Spirit, and he was the *kerux* of the Lord. On his way to Rome, he was shipwrecked on the island of Malta, and while building a fire a snake fastened to his hand (Acts 28:3). The islanders thought Paul was going to die, but he shook the snake off (the meaning of "taking up serpents" in Mark 16:18). Why? Paul knew the Lord said he would stand before Caesar; as a result, the attack of the serpent would not supersede the Word of the Lord. Paul demonstrated the sign of preservation. Additionally, Paul manifested other supernatural gifts of healing and miracles. What would have happened if Paul would have become overwhelmed with his circumstances? What if he would have been distraught and angry with being shipwrecked or fear-driven by a snakebite? Paul was in the flow of the Spirit; he didn't allow the natural realm to overshadow the spiritual realm, and he remained at rest in the presence of God. As a result, he was not only preserved through shipwreck and snakebite, but he was in the spiritual condition to release the presence of God upon the island.

Time and space does not permit me to list the martyrs through history who "wouldn't die" before their appointed time. They remained intimate with God and rested in the Spirit, and many saw the sign of preservation. Moreover, Jesus ended up drinking the cup of deadly poison for everyone, and He triumphed over death by the power of God. This is the sign of preservation. I hope you know by now I'm not suggesting that you taunt a snake or drink poison to test the Lord. But a Spirit-filled believer who walks in intimacy with Jesus doesn't need to fear death; they can fulfill Jesus' assignment of preaching to the world in total peace. David said "I will fear no evil" in Psalm 23:4 because he walked in intimacy with the Lord. Should we, who have the Holy Spirit, live any different?

Fourth, Jesus mentioned the sign of restoration when he said "they will lay hands on the sick, and they will recover" (Mark 16:18). When you minister out of intimacy, you will release the presence of Christ that is on you and in you, and people will be restored. My friend Dan Bohi was preaching at a district camp, and after an evening service, he started ministering as the Spirit led him. I was three feet away from a woman who got out of a wheelchair after ten years of confinement. Another friend of mine came to my church to minister, and as she preached and talked about the gospel, she laid hands on someone who had severely injured their back many years earlier. It was almost a crippling injury, yet when my friend laid hands on them, they were instantly healed of all pain. A man in my church had someone lay hands on him, and he was healed from twenty years of asthma and food allergies. All praise to God for each of these victories and many more that I've personally witnessed.

I could go on, but my point is that these signs follow those who believe. We don't chase after the signs, but they seem to follow us when we remain in the Spirit. When you minister out of intimacy with Christ, hearing His words and releasing His words, your life will make a difference in the world around you. "Now to Him who is able to do exceedingly abundantly above all that we ask or think, according to the power that works in us" (Eph. 3:20).

Following the Voice

Living and functioning by the voice of the Spirit is exhilarating; you are always poised to respond to the slightest promptings. I can't begin to count the times I've sensed the Lord speaking to me to say or do something that resulted in God touching another person. Sometimes they prayed to receive Christ, other times I simply expressed God's love, still other times God led me to pray for their healing of a particular need. When we're resting in His presence and poised to respond to His voice, significant things will happen through us.

A friend of mine is seeing Muslims converted because he simply helps them listen to the voice. How is that possible? If we believe in the active presence of the Holy Spirit, then we should expect Him to move and speak when we entreat and invoke His presence. This guy simply says to these Muslims, "If *my* God is real, then He can and will speak to you if you listen." And sure enough, the Holy Spirit starts to manifest upon these Muslims, and they realize Christianity and Christ is real! Life is in His voice, and my friend is following that voice and leading others to Jesus.

As we were beginning to learn the importance of being sensitive to His presence and following the voice of the Spirit, we had an intern at our church. He went into a coffee shop in our city, and while talking with the young lady who owned the shop, he noticed that she leaned in with her right ear. He realized after a while that she was deaf in her left ear. Later that night, the Spirit of the Lord began speaking to him about this lady, and God asked him to pray for her the next day. However, the Lord gave him more information about why she was deaf. The next day he went to the coffee shop and asked for permission to pray for her. He prayed a simple prayer for her ear to be healed, but he also prayed that she would be healed from the tragedy and abuse that caused the injury.

The fact is, earlier in her life she had been terribly abused by a man. He locked her in the bathroom, beat her, and punched her so hard that her ear was permanently damaged. She finally managed to break free of that abusive situation but, in fear, told no one about it. She attempted to recover the best she could and move on with life, and years later, she purchased a coffee shop. Then out of nowhere, in walks a guy who was simply leaning into the voice of the Spirit; a *kerux* stepped into that coffee shop. His prayer for this precious lady's healing was answered on both accounts. Within hours, she was talking on the phone and asked the person to stop yelling. Then she realized that she was holding the phone to her left ear, and her hearing was completely restored. Moreover, her heart was healed and set free from the trauma and pain of her abuse. She opened her heart up to the presence of Christ, and now is serving the Lord with a passion. I recently spoke with her and was blessed by her faithfulness in pursuing the Lord.

I wonder how many people we bypass because we're distracted and consumed by this earthly realm. It breaks my heart to think about the untouched people in our world who desperately need a *kerux* to pass by. There are many people who need healing, salvation, deliverance, hope, restoration, and sometimes, they simply need to be loved. Jesus is the answer, but He wants to flow through you and me — ordinary people who are saturated with His Spirit accomplishing extraordinary things by His Spirit.

Chapter Ten

The Supernatural and Suffering

———∾∾∾———

L iving a life in the Word and the Spirit is never more imperative than when you walk through pain. Supernatural
experiences are real and life-changing, but so is suffering.
A book examining a topic like ours wouldn't be complete
without attempting to discuss the tension between the supernatural and suffering. So I'll share my story.

The first year after my sabbatical, the constant and consistent outpouring of God's Holy Spirit exceeded anything
I had ever experienced or witnessed previously. A Spirit of
revelation fell on so many in our church and we grew spiritually; the Holy Spirit taught us so much, just as the Bible says
(1 John 2:27). Miracles were not only happening inside the
walls of our church, but God was using us outside the walls,
and supernatural activities were taking place almost weekly.
By late summer of that same year, we felt prompted to have
a healing service. In all my years of ministry, I couldn't
think of one single time I had attempted a healing service.
It's amazing how we drift from doing the activities that Jesus
did—and commissioned us to do. If Word and Spirit are not
part of your theology, then they won't be part of your practice.
I had always preached the Word of God, but I didn't have a
paradigm for the functioning power of the Spirit. But all of

that changed after the Holy Spirit started moving powerfully in our church. So I scheduled a healing service for the last Sunday of October in 2007.

September of that year began with no less fervor. We were two months away from a healing service, and we were planning to pray for people to be healed spiritually, emotionally, and physically. I realized that the redemptive power of God was able to touch all three of those aspects in our life (see 1 Thess. 5:23). The excitement and anticipation was building within our congregation. In the midst of our plans, my wife, Cindy, had a routine mammogram scheduled the first week into September. There were no immediate concerns other than an area that she believed needed a second look. The doctor suggested a biopsy, so needless to say our minds and thoughts became overwhelmed. We elicited the prayer support from a few people who knew about the exam and expected a clean report, especially in the wake of all the miracles we were seeing.

Then, the phone call came that no one wants to receive, on her birthday, no less. The doctor called and said that Cindy had breast cancer. She hung the phone up, and we wept and cried out to God together.

I wish that I could tell you that living in the supernatural meant that there would be no suffering. I wish I could say that if you united the Word and the Spirit, you would never walk through difficulties. But there is such a mystery to the supernatural, and many books have been written on the subject of being in the presence of God and in the presence of pain at the same time.

To be honest, the days that followed that phone call were some of the most challenging days we have ever walked through. You can't avoid having hard conversations with each other concerning life—and death. You can't avoid talking about the "what if's." We did our share of crying together, and we spent many sleepless nights staring at the ceiling trying to make sense of it all. Most of all, we prayed! And we prayed for healing. We prayed for the specific area that the doctors identified to be healed. Cindy was anointed; we fasted and prayed and expected nothing less than another miracle. The doctor had scheduled Cindy to have a mastectomy within a few weeks of the diagnosis. There was one last ultrasound before the surgery, and we believed that the doctor was going to announce that the tumor was gone.

The ultrasound revealed the tumor was still there, and so surgery continued as scheduled. Then I received the call I didn't want to get; in the midst of her surgery, the doctor called me and explained that the cancer had reached into the lymph nodes. At that point, I was not sure as to what extent the cancer had spread throughout her body, so I found a quiet place at the hospital where I could simply "sit at the feet" of Jesus to hear His voice.

The Lines of Demarcation

There is such a mystery to this whole subject, and no one really has all of the answers biblically, theologically, or scientifically. Moreover, answers were not what I needed at that moment. I needed God's grace; I needed the embrace of His presence, and that is exactly what I experienced as I sat at His feet. I felt safe under the shadow of the Almighty.

He clothed us with grace as we learned that the cancer was contained to one lymph node, and He sustained us with grace as we walked through six months of chemotherapy. The whole process was about a year long, and at the end of that season, Cindy had full body scans to see if the cancer was eliminated. We praise God that they found no trace of cancer anywhere in her body, and today she is a picture of health and beauty. I realize that the happy ending to our story is different from others. At my age, I've watched many people make their journey through enormous pain, and their ending was not what they had prayed for. For us, our season of suffering was no walk in the park. As I look back, I'm able to draw a few lessons that are noteworthy. I call these lessons lines of demarcation; they were "make or break" decisions for Cindy and me and for our ongoing ministry.

First, my immediate prayer from the moment that we learned about the cancer was the same: "God, I want Cindy healed." The evening of her surgery, when I learned that the cancer had gone into her lymph nodes, I considered the outcome. When I found a quiet place at the hospital to pray and seek the Lord, my prayer was the same plea—I wanted her to be healed. This time God spoke clearly to me with these unforgettable words: "I want you to love Me more than you want Cindy to live." I knew that God wanted to be, and had to be, the first priority in my life, and my desire to see her live could not replace my love for God. So that night I surrendered Cindy to God, and I consecrated my life to Him anew, regardless of what the outcome would be. Our relationship to God can never be contingent upon results that we are praying for. He is looking to "show Himself strong" to those who are fully devoted to Him (2 Chron. 16:9). Freedom comes only to those who relinquish everything to God, and when I gave up, I experienced a sustaining peace that has never left me to this day. That is a huge lesson that we all have to learn; it's a game-changer, too. Have you honestly given God everything?

Second, I made the declaration that God is good and the devil is bad, and I never got that confused. That sounds like an elementary lesson, but if we think for one second that God is punishing us or He's trying to "get us back" for something we did wrong in the past or He's making us sick to teach us something, we'll never fully trust Him. I can emphatically say that God didn't give Cindy cancer, and He certainly didn't give it to her to teach us a lesson. The Bible says that it is the enemy that comes as a thief to steal, kill, and destroy

(John 10:10). The painful circumstances, loss, cancer, disease, sickness, or whatever might try to damage or destroy God's temple are the enemy's plan; but our lives will always be used to bring glory to God. J. Kenneth Grider, my theology professor at Nazarene Theological Seminary, often said, "God doesn't 'will' everything that happens to us, but God's 'will' can be discovered *in* everything that happens to us." So I don't believe that God *willed* cancer upon Cindy, but His will was discovered in the midst of our adversity. We discovered His nearness, peace, and guidance; His presence overshadowed us, and His grace was sufficient every moment.

Beyond that, we refused to speak complaints or laments. Our mouths became the instruments of praise to God through those long, grueling weeks of chemotherapy. We played worship music in our house every day, night and day. The resounding testimony on our lips was, "the Lord is good; and His love endures forever." We began to make biblical declarations over our lives; we activated the Word, and the Spirit ministered to our hearts.

This leads me to the third lesson that I learned, we refused to allow a spirit of offense to capture us. The Greek word "offense" (*skandalizo*) means to trap, or to cause someone to stumble. Praising God through difficult circumstances kept us from getting trapped and embittered. John the Baptist was in prison because of his boldness in preaching. The circumstances must have been difficult for him because he sent a couple of his disciples to Jesus asking this question: "Are you the Coming One?" Remember that John preached with conviction that Jesus was the Lamb of God who takes away the sin of the world; he was the forerunner to Jesus, and when he saw the Lord he acknowledged Him before the crowds. But now in this dark prison, John started to question in his mind some things he had believed about Jesus. His despair has caused him to ask some crucial questions about Jesus the Messiah.

When John's disciples asked the question, Jesus response to them was, "Go and tell John the things you have seen and heard: that the blind see, the lame walk, the lepers are cleansed, the deaf hear, the dead are raised, the poor have the gospel preached to them" (Luke 7:22). "Yes" Jesus said, "Miracles are still happening—I'm the anointed Messiah." Jesus was very clear; He wanted John to know that He was the Miracle Maker, the Coming One. But just before John's disciples turned to leave, Jesus added one more comment, "And blessed is he who is not *offended* because of Me [emphasis mine]" (v. 23). In other words, "Tell John that I'm still the Messiah no matter what happens to him. He must not become trapped by what I may or may not do." The fact that John was in prison didn't change the truth of who Jesus is. His messianic position was not altered by John's earthly circumstances. In spite of the fact that Cindy had cancer, Jesus is still the Lord of lords and the King of kings; He's still the Miracle Maker! Nothing changed that fact in our minds, so we refused to become offended by earthly circumstances.

Let me tell you this: no matter what you might be experiencing this minute in your life, Jesus is still the Messiah. He's still the worker of miracles; He's still the Lord. Don't allow circumstances to become larger than God, or you will become offended with Him. He's bigger than your "prison," and He's still the Lord no matter your results. Trust Him regardless of what He may or may not do. Job's cry was the correct response, "Though He slay me, yet will I trust Him" (13:15). After David lamented God's silence and the enemy's triumphs, he relinquished himself to the Lord with this: "But I have trusted in Your mercy; my heart shall rejoice in Your salvation" (Ps. 13:5). You can always trust God.

The final lesson I learned is that my experience cannot govern the Word of God. Sometimes disappointments lead us to lower the Word of God to our experiences, and we rewrite doctrines that fit the context of what we're going through. We conclude that healing or miracles are not for today because we haven't experienced any or because we prayed for someone and they were not healed. History records the disappointment that Thomas Jefferson, the third President of the United States, experienced when his wife died. The death of his wife led him to cut out the pages of Scripture that cited all of the miracles of Jesus and any mention of the supernatural, thus leaving a condensed composition of the Bible. The Bible is in the Smithsonian National Museum of American History, and it is a testimony of his views and beliefs that emerged out of his disappointment. His views and beliefs have been carried on through humanists and many universities to this day.

I don't have explanations for why God touches some people in miraculous ways and why others remain diseased or crippled. I can't answer why people were being healed in our church, but Cindy had to endure surgery and chemotherapy. I do know that I cannot allow what I don't understand about the miraculous to supersede what the Bible says. Jesus told us to heal the sick; the Bible says in James that the prayer of faith will save the sick. Every person who came to Jesus and needed to be healed was miraculously touched. Jesus never turned anyone away or told them that God was teaching them a lesson. Jesus is my pattern; I expect the same results every time I pray. I'm not going to cut those pages out of the Bible. I want to elevate my experiences to the standard of the Bible rather than lower the Bible to my limited experiences.

Remember the healing service that we had scheduled for the end of October? The night that I learned from the doctor that cancer had spread to Cindy's lymph nodes, I had no idea what the final outcome would be. I didn't know if Cindy would live or die, but as I prayed and sought God late into that night I realized that the Word of God prevailed over my circumstances. I realized that it would have been a mistake to cancel our healing service because of our situation. I couldn't allow my earthly experience to trump God's Word.

157

So we kept the healing service on the schedule as planned, and God demonstrated His power by touching people spiritually, emotionally, and physically. That service, the last Sunday of October, was filled with testimonies of people being saved, healed physically, sanctified, and delivered from many strongholds.

I don't mean to sound overdramatic, but had I back-peddled and succumb to fear and offense and whittled God's Word down to our circumstances I would have stunted my spiritual progress. There is something extraordinary about walking through adversity and still believing in the supernatural. God seems to favor those who believe Him for things that are contradictory to the immediate circumstances they find themselves in.

Trusting the Word of the Lord

In Luke 5, Jesus taught the multitudes from a boat. When He stopped, He turned to Simon Peter and said, "Launch out into the deep and let down your nets for a catch" (v. 4). Jesus spoke a specific word to Simon Peter, yet Simon explained to Jesus that they had been toiling all night and caught nothing. In other words, Simon was responding from his limited experience; he wanted Jesus to realize that from his perspective, launching out into the deep to catch fish would be of no benefit. Allow me to insert the following: I've prayed about that before; I've put my faith in that and it didn't work; I've sought God about that situation and got no response; or, I've asked for healing and it didn't happen. These are typical responses that we might explain to Jesus should He prompt us to do something that is outside the parameters of our experience.

I have had people explain to me that they've gone to the altar during an invitation, seeking to be healed, and nothing happened to them. So they believe that God has changed His mind on the issue of healing. Bob Sorge said belief in God's

Word to heal gives him the incentive and momentum to continue pursuing God.[133] Sorge has been waiting and trusting God for his own healing but refuses to quit pursuing God on the matter because of what the Bible says. My friend Craig Rench told me about a woman who went forward to be healed fifty times and nothing happened to her, but on the fifty-first time she was instantly healed. We must always trust God's word over our circumstances, no matter how long we have labored.

Simon Peter conceded, tossing the net overboard, and it was filled with more fish than it could hold. Simon fell at Jesus' feet in repentance realizing that he could have missed the blessing if he had failed to obey Jesus. There is an interesting bit of insight to this story that is worth mentioning. Some translations state that Jesus told Simon Peter to let down the "nets" (*diktua*) which is a plural, yet Simon only cast out one "net" (*diktoun*), a singular noun. It would appear that Simon, in his reluctance to trust Jesus' Word, only partially obeyed Jesus, and he adjusted Jesus' words to fit his lack of faith. In that case, Simon *really* missed a blessing. We can only imagine the amount of fish he would have caught had there been three or four nets in the water. If we allow our experiences to define what is possible, then we'll miss what God might want to do. We must not reduce the Word or redefine it to fit our context. The Word of God will always trump our experiences if we trust Him.

Think about Joseph who persevered from the time of promise to the time of fulfillment. The Bible says, "Until the time that His word came to pass, the word of the Lord tested him" (Ps. 105:19). From the point of receiving the promise of God's Word, Joseph experienced the pit, Potiphar, prison, and eventually the palace. But for thirteen long years, he never lost sight of God's Word. His life of "ups and downs" was experienced *because* he trusted the Word of the Lord, and the Word tested him. Jesus explained that tribulation and persecution arises because of the Word (Matt. 13:21). So we must believe the Word of the Lord over the circumstances that testify to something different, knowing that the conflict is arising to challenge our faith. Sometimes we'll never know the strength of the Word until we sense the strength of the opposition, but if we remain faithful to His Word, it enhances the blessings when fulfillment comes.

The worship leader in our church has a son who was born with a condition where the blood vessels around his brain would start to bleed, and he would have seizures. This condition prevented him from running and playing like most children because the cardiovascular activity would cause pressure on the small capillaries, bleeding, and subsequent seizures. When she and her husband learned of this condition, we started praying. We believed that God would heal him. Every six months they took him to Children's Hospital in Columbus, Ohio, for an MRI. We prayed and laid hands on him, but the MRI reported the same results. This pattern occurred for nine years, and for nine years we continued to trust God's Word. For nine long years, we sought God, we prayed, we fasted, and we declared the Word over the situation. Then one Sunday, my friend came to preach for us, and before he taught, he said that he had a word of knowledge for these parents. He said that God had told him whatever condition their son was in, he was going to be "normal." Two weeks later, a stunned doctor gave the report to this couple that their son was normal. Today he is part of our worship team and lives a normal life.

I have learned through our own pain, and by seeing others persevere through difficult seasons in their life, that God is the God of breakthrough (2 Sam. 5:20). His Word will not return void, but will prosper in the thing for which it was sent (Isa. 55:11). We must never allow disappointing experiences and circumstances that didn't end well to redefine doctrine for us. Nothing is impossible for those who believe, so place your faith in His Word and not your experiences.

The Power of Perseverance

So what about those who don't get the breakthrough that they are crying out for? No one can hide the fact that sometimes adversity seems to win with untimely deaths or tragic accidents. A young couple in our church learned that they were expecting their third child. Several months into the pregnancy, doctors informed them of complications with the baby and advised them to abort. Should the baby be born, doctors said, it would never live. The couple prayed and trusted God. Our church rallied behind them with prayer support. When the baby was born, he was a beautiful boy, and he *did* live but only for five hours. Several of us prayed for a resurrection, but instead, we experienced a funeral. Yet, this family persevered. They worshipped at the funeral and praised God for enduring grace. I have rarely seen such devotion to God as I saw in this couple. God has manifested through this family in multiple ways since then, and today the husband is studying to enter into full-time ministry. They named their son who lived only five hours Chance Miracle, because those five hours superseded any expectation that doctors could possibly envision. This family still believes in the supernatural and miracles, too. Their experience has not jaded them or led them to redefine biblical truths. If anything, it has propelled them to chase Jesus with a greater intensity. Their story is a demonstration of the power of perseverance.

Disease, pain, sickness, and sorrows enter into our lives either directly or indirectly by the enemy. The enemy desires to destroy our lives, and ultimately our souls. Yet, in the midst of the valley of weeping—if we will persevere—the valley will become a fountain of life (Ps. 84:6). Where the enemy longs to harm us, the Holy Spirit will engage us and teach us. We learn, while walking through adversity, how to walk, Sorge said, with "extreme caution, humility, brokenness, and implicit dependence upon God."[134] Those kinds of lesson are forged in some of life's most difficult circumstances. The weakness that we feel during times of sorrow is an invitation for the Spirit to camp out upon our lives and demonstrate His power.

Paul made a very interesting statement in 2 Corinthians 12:9, "I will rather boast in my infirmities, that the power of Christ may rest upon me." Who would trumpet their weaknesses? Paul did because he learned that the supernatural power (*dunamis*) of God rested (*episkenoo*, which means to fix a tent upon someone) upon someone in their weakness. Adversity has a way of setting the stage for a demonstration of the power of God. It's as if the supernatural God "shows off" in times when we would least expect. As my prayer partner always says, when the enemy believes that we're down to nothing, that's when God demonstrates that He's up to something!

Many scholars point to the fact that Paul endured a "thorn" in his flesh for a while. We don't know how long Paul was challenged by this obstacle, but we do know two things. First, the thorn was a messenger (literally an angel, i.e., demon) of Satan sent to destroy Paul (2 Cor. 12:7). I've heard a lot of interpretations over the years as to what exactly this thorn was. But I'm comfortable with letting the Bible speak for itself; Satan wanted to "buffet" Paul. This word is *kolaphizo*, and it means to beat with one's fist so as to destroy someone. There is no doubt that the enemy wanted to destroy Paul. The second thing that we know is that God told Paul His grace was sufficient (v. 9). This meant more than "hang in there" or "keep a stiff upper lip" as you walk through trials. James Garlow said, "Grace is God's willingness to unleash His power on our behalf even though we don't deserve it."[135] Grace is not something merely believed in but is something that is experienced: a divine force, a transforming power.[136] Paul was given the *power* to confront the enemy that threatened him, and that power gave him the ability to persevere and later write at the end of his life, "I have kept the faith" (2 Tim. 4:7).

I certainly can't promise that we will experience the kind of breakthrough that we desire. But I have learned that if we'll persevere with God's grace, somehow it opens the doors to supernatural results in our lives. Additionally, we are never more of a detriment to the enemy than when we honor and praise God through suffering. Cindy and I use to say that our worship to God, in spite of how we felt at the time or what our immediate circumstances were, was our divine retribution toward the enemy. I remember reading those profound words by C. S. Lewis, a satire of two demons talking, when a superior demon named Screwtape laments to his nephew. Screwtape was disconcerted about Christians who faithfully served God even when they sensed His absence. He wrote to his nephew these words: "Our cause is never more in danger than when a human, no longer desiring, but still intending, to do our enemy's (God) will, looks round upon a universe from which every trace of him seems to have vanished, and asks why he has been forsaken, and still obeys."[137] That mindset represents the power of perseverance, and it not only exhibits the power of God, but it wreaks havoc on the kingdom of darkness.

Those long weeks of chemotherapy and all that they entailed are forever etched in our minds. Yet, in the midst of it all, Cindy and I grew more tenacious in our pursuit of God. We longed for His manifest presence, we sought His Word, and we worshipped the Lord with an ever-increasing fervor. We walked by faith, and somehow God not only rested upon us, but He manifested through us in supernatural ways. Beyond that, our experience has embedded into our hearts the power to persevere. If we should ever endure a situation where breakthrough this side of eternity does not occur, I pray that we would boast in our weakness like Paul and discover just how sufficient God's grace can be in our refusal to quit trusting and obeying Him.

Changing the Atmosphere

I once heard the former president of Asbury College Dennis Kinlaw speak on the subject of affecting the atmosphere around us by releasing what is inside us. He referenced a speaker at the college who stood before an audience with a glass of water in their hands, and the speaker asked someone to come forward and shake his arm. Of course, when the speaker's arm was shaken water spilled all over the floor. The speaker asked, "So why did water spill?" Everyone answered the obvious that the speaker's arm had been shaken. He asked the question again with a bit of emphasis: "Why did *water* spill?" People caught on and then answered: "Because water was in the glass." Kinlaw went on to explain that what spilled out of the glass was not determined by the shaking, but what spilled out was determined by what actually was in the glass. If the speaker held a glass of milk, then milk would have spilled on the floor. If juice was in the glass, then juice is what would have spilled on the floor.

So what spills from our life is never determined by the amount of shaking, what spills from our lives is determined by what we are filled with. Difficulties along the way, things that rattle us, adversity, trials and suffering are all things that merely reveal what we're full of. It's the reason, Kinlaw stressed, that every Christian must be completely filled with and walking in the power of the Holy Spirit. Jesus said, "He who believes in Me, as the Scriptures has said, out of his heart will flow rivers of living water" (John 7:38). I desire to be so filled with His Spirit that His Spirit is what gets released whenever I'm shaken.

After several trips to chemotherapy, Cindy and I realized that we could affect the atmosphere at the hospital by what possessed us, namely, the Holy Spirit. It dawned on us that we could release the Spirit if we remained sensitive to His leadership. So we started praying over people while they were receiving chemotherapy treatments along with Cindy. In my mind, I can still see Cindy's thin body and wig-clad head standing beside other ladies, laying hands on them and praying for their healing as they both were receiving treatments. We saw people touched and encouraged; we were able to "spill Jesus" upon people and see lives changed amidst our adversity.

When you and I walk across a threshold and enter a room, we have the blessed privilege and assignment to gush forth with the Holy Spirit. I believe the entire atmosphere in an area can shift because of the rivers of living water—the Holy Spirit—that is being poured out of our heart. It doesn't matter the conditions around us. We will release what we're filled with, and if we're saturated with the Holy Spirit, His Spirit is going to be released. The New Testament believers demonstrated that kind of lifestyle. They were persecuted, flogged, and mistreated, yet the joy of the Lord was released. Everywhere that they went, they released the presence of the Spirit because they remained saturated in Him; their lifestyle of intimacy affected Jews and Gentiles alike. Entire families were converted and whole cities transformed, all because these primitive believers remained immersed in the Spirit and the Spirit is what they spilled out wherever they journeyed.

By now I hope you realize that a supernatural lifestyle is not about pursuing gifts, signs, and miracles. Those things are the overflow of a life of intimacy with Christ; the product of walking in the Spirit and increasing in the Spirit. We should be made aware of gifts, and we should be instructed in the supernatural. Those things should be included in the curriculum of colleges and seminaries. Additionally, the supernatural lifestyle should be inclusive in discipling new believers—it certainly was part of Jesus' method of discipling. But when the dust of the supernatural settles, I hope you realize that living for and in His presence is the real essence of New Testament Christianity.

My challenge to you is to live from a position of intimacy with Christ; walk in the Spirit, and continue to increase in the Spirit. If you do, then regardless of what you might walk through, no matter how you might suffer, in spite of the difficulties that "shake" you, the contents of your life will affect the atmosphere around you. Your life of undistracted intimacy in the presence of Christ will affect a world. You will spill His Spirit; you will demonstrate to a world the lifestyle of Jesus, a life dedicated to the Word and the Spirit.

Conclusion

The More Excellent Way

There's a minister who travels around the world and is known for his incredible prophetic anointing. Moreover, he has experienced extraordinary miracles in his meetings. However, while he was ministering with some close friends of mine, he was rude, demanding, and indignant with them and the hosts of the conference. I thought perhaps that he might have been going through a difficult time in his life only to learn through firsthand experience that he repeated the same kind of behavior at another conference. People may not remember how anointed someone's ministry is, but they most certainly will remember how they were treated by the one doing the ministry. Jesus condensed the Law and the Prophets down to this simple command: Love God and love people (Matt. 22:37–40). There is no greater calling for Christian people than to love; truly, nothing is more like Jesus than becoming a person of love.

No doubt when the Word and the Spirit are united in our lives, we will replicate Jesus' lifestyle. Also, a supernatural lifestyle is a natural lifestyle for those who remain intimate with Jesus; in other words, we'll reflect the nature of the One we're intimate with. We have examined the supernatural manifestations that are the result of being possessed by the

Holy Spirit. I've attempted to emphasize that theology, education, and discipleship should be inclusive of the Word and the Spirit, and if that happens, our lives will personify the life of Jesus as did the primitive New Testament believers. But in the final analysis, I believe that nothing is more Christlike and nothing will leave a greater touch—the most lasting impression—upon people than when we become love to them.

After Paul described a supernatural culture where the Holy Spirit manifested for the profit of the entire body of Christ, he transitioned into a chapter that has affectionately been called the "Love Chapter." In 1 Corinthians 12:31, Paul began his discourse as he wrote to the Corinthians that he was going to "show [them] a more excellent way." Suffice to say that the "more excellent way" that Paul talked about was a description of something that is beyond comparison or beyond measure. It was not a lifestyle void of the supernatural gifts, but a supernatural lifestyle expressed in a more excellent way. If the manifestations are going to make the greatest impact, they must flow from a person possessed of love.

I hope we don't ever get lost in the rhetoric of theology and doctrine; and I hope we don't spend too much energy arguing over gifts, graces, signs, and wonders. Even our discussion of Word and Spirit, while imperative, cannot overshadow this simple truth that God is love (1 John 4:8), and to be most like Him we must manifest love to a broken, love-deficient world. The Bible says the following about love: Love is the greatest commandment (Matt. 22:37–39), love is the distinguishing characteristic of being Jesus' follower (John 13:35), love is the sweet-smelling fragrance of Christ (Eph. 5:2), love is the bond of perfection (Col. 3:14), and love never fails (1 Cor. 13:8). If you really want to see what a life of the Word and the Spirit looks like, look no further than someone who is a lover of God and a lover of people.

What *is* love? How is it defined? You need to realize that the term is washed out in our culture because we say things like "I love my wife" and "I love my dog," hopefully in that order, too. But what does it mean to love? Unlike the English language, which has only one word for "love," the Greek language has four different words.

First, is the word *eros,* which is defined as a sexual, erotic type of love. However, this word is never used in the Bible, not even in the context of sexual intimacy between a husband and wife. The root idea behind this word is selfish gratification, and it's far from what God calls us to. Second is the word *stergo,* which is a relational love as seen in a family. It's used rarely in the Bible, and where we find this type of love, it's depicted in a negative manner. For example, in 2 Timothy 3:3, *stergo* is defined as being unloving. Third is the word *phileo,* which describes the affection between two people. This word is used several places in the New Testament and usually it depicts the love between friends. *Phileo* is usually used as a compound word that describes the love of something specific, for example: the love of our brother (*philadelphia*), the love of wisdom (*philosophia*), or the love of strangers (*philoxenos*).

The final word is *agape,* and the meaning of this word, which is used in the New Testament, defines the love of God. This type of love is only generated by God; it defines who God is—He is love (*agape*). We cannot actuate this kind of love without being filled with God's Spirit. There is no way to manufacture *agape* through our own efforts. We experience His love first, and then He enables us to give it away to others.

Over the years I've read many definitions of this kind of love, but no definition has touched me more than this one:

> *Agape* love occurs when an individual sees, recognizes, understands, or appreciates the value of another person, causing the viewer to behold this person in great esteem, awe, admiration, wonder, and sincere appreciation. Such

> great respect is awakened in the heart of the
> observer for the person he is beholding that he
> is compelled to love them. In fact, his love for
> that person is so strong that it is irresistible....
> when you love with this kind of love, it is
> impossible for you to feel hurt or let down by
> the response of the recipients of your love.[138]

The line that really underscores *agape* love is "it is impossible for you to feel hurt or let down by the response of the recipients of your love." This kind of love is not contingent upon others responding favorably toward you. If you truly love someone with *agape* love, you aren't seeking anything from them. Your only thought is to pour love upon them because you are so full of Jesus. Your heart is engaged in giving no matter how you're treated. There are no conditions attached to this kind of love.

After three years of pouring His life out for others, the very people that Jesus touched, healed, cleansed, and cured turned on Him and crucified Him. Yet, Jesus didn't retaliate. He didn't complain to the Father by saying "life isn't fair." We can't even picture Jesus getting mad at the jeering crowds during His crucifixion and saying hurtful things about them. If we can't imagine Jesus doing that, it should be just as difficult to imagine Spirit-filled believers responding any differently. Jesus forgave the angry mobs because He loved them, and He realized that they had no idea what they were doing. That response is the nature of *agape* love; it compels us to lay down our life for other people regardless of what they say or do to us. You simply love others; no questions, no expectations, no reservations, or no strings attached. Because God has loved you, you are enabled to love others, and because God's love is unlimited, your love for others reflects that same characteristic.

The fact is, Jesus loved people who were incapable of reciprocating His love. Yet, He loved them anyway. Our call is to demonstrate this love to a fallen world, but keep in mind that those whom we love will often be incapable of returning *agape* love. Moreover, I would argue that even in the Church, people have skewed understandings of love. So when you love someone who persecutes you or love someone who maligns your character or love someone who takes advantage of you, you are bestowing the essence of the supernatural. The heart of the supernatural lifestyle is love—we are to be compelled by love (2 Cor. 5:14). If we love others, we will never adjust our attitude based on what people do to us because our attitude has been aligned with Christ's (Phil. 2:5). Jesus descended into greatness; we only rise higher by going lower, by humbling ourselves and loving others regardless of how we're treated.

In some ways, nothing is more miraculous than *agape* love. When you love with His love, you are impervious to being hurt by people. Why? Because to truly love with *agape* love, you are dead! In other words, your life has been crucified with Christ and He lives through you (Gal. 2:20). So you give, you pray, you sacrifice, you forgive, you heal, you minister, and you simply don't think of yourself anymore. Your life is a funnel that God's incredible love is poured through. This kind of love changed our world two-thousand years ago when Jesus declared, "It is finished" (John 19:30). We have the blessed privilege to extend that same kind of love all over our world.

A missionary who was in my cohort has a wife who personifies love. They minister to poor, impoverished people in a remote part of the world. It's not uncommon for the wife to cradle sick, diseased, dirty children in her arms for hours until the healing power of Jesus cures them. One time she held a woman with no eyes, who was abandoned by her parents. After a while, two beautiful brown eyes were formed in the woman that she held. While most of us marvel over these miracles, these missionaries desire greater love still. They've learned that the supernatural is the byproduct of *agape* love being released in the atmosphere. Otherwise, without authentic love, we become charlatans with cheap parlor tricks and street magic.

Who can forget Jesus' words to those who performed mighty miracles in His name, but they were not intimate with Him (Matt. 7:22–23)? Jesus told them to depart from Him. They used His name to invoke a response, but they really didn't know the heart of Jesus. To know Jesus is to know love, and the more time you spend with Him, the deeper your love for people will be. Stated differently, the depth of your love for others is to the proportion of your intimacy with Christ.

The greatest impartation that we can give is *agape* love because it is eternal. In fact, according to Paul, the supernatural gifts will accomplish nothing without love. People are touched the deepest by His love. Love is what will leave the most lasting impression upon people, irrespective of how explosive we've been in the Spirit.

More than anything else, I want to live so much like Jesus that I'm described as a lover. When you reunite Word and Spirit, it looks exactly like Jesus. When you look at Jesus, you discover a picture of love. My prayer for the Holiness movement, and for churches in all denominations, is that our lives will be the fusion of the Word and the Spirit. However, our mark on history will probably not be described by those terms, but by the incredible, unceasing, extraordinary, profound nature of God's love that was poured from our lives. It is the more excellent way.

Appendix One

A Response to Cessationism

—*০∿০*—

This is a brief response to cessationism, specifically, how I would respond to someone who would challenge my believing in the ongoing supernatural gifts (*charismata*). Cessationism is the belief that miraculous spiritual gifts, including prophecy, were in some sense "foundational" in that they were essential for the initiation and spread of the Christian faith, but like scaffolding, they were no longer required after the viable structure and doctrines of the church had been established. A cessationist would claim that at the end of the apostolic age, all *charismata*, prophetic leadings, signs, and wonders had ceased.

How would I defend my position against cessationism? What would I say in response to someone who claims to be a cessationist? Honestly, my initial thought would be to invite them to pray with me, believing that the "kingdom of God is not in word but in power" (1 Cor. 4:20), and trust that they would be seized by the power of the Holy Spirit. If that didn't work, I would give them a great book by a guy I know who specifically addresses a Protestant polemic on post-biblical miracles (Jon Mark Ruthven's book, *The Cessation of the Charismata*). But should I revert to mere debate and convincing on my own, I would offer the following thoughts.

- The Bible states that the *charismata* will not be taken away in Romans 11:29. Paul used a word that literally means irrevocable. Simply put, when God gives gifts, they will never be withdrawn. Note that this is a universal declaration and generalization—not for a specific, limited situation.

- The Bible says we will not come short of *any* gift as we wait for the revelation of our Lord Jesus Christ in 1 Corinthians 1:7–8. The point here is that gifts, spiritual utterance, and revelatory knowledge are installments until we are presented before the Lord at the end of the age.

- In 1 Corinthians 12:6, Paul said that "God works all the gifts in all people." *The Good News Bible* says, "The same God produces every gift in every person." All of the gifts are being worked in all of God's people, not just the apostles or for a certain period of time.

- In 1 Corinthians 13:8–13, Paul argued for the eternal quality of *agape* love, stating that charismatic gifts will no longer be necessary when Jesus Christ returns. *When* we see Christ face to face, *then*, the *charismata* (prophecies, tongues, knowledge) will vanish, but not until then. This passage actually underscores the permanent availability of the gifts in this age.

- Paul stated his concerns for God's people in the last days by identifying some troubling issues, but the most concerning issue seems to be the fact that believers will have a form of godliness while denying its power in 2 Timothy 3:5. The word for "deny" literally means to disavow or reject something that has been given. Rejecting the *dunamis* (God's miraculous power) is what a cessationist seems to do with post-biblical believers. However, Jesus said that when we are filled with the Holy Spirit, we will receive *dunamis* power (Acts 1:8), and there is no expiration date to that divine unction. Moreover, that power should manifest through any Spirit-filled believer as witnessed in the book of Acts; unless, of course, a person adopts a cessationist position and accepts merely a form of Christianity with no anointing.

- The Old Testament prophet, Joel, prophesied that God's Spirit would be poured out upon all flesh, and men and women would prophesy (Joel 2:28). Peter echoed that statement at Pentecost, the inauguration of the New Covenant. We're in the last days, and the Spirit is still being poured out. In fact, we're told by Jesus that we can have more of the Spirit (Luke 11:13), and Paul indicated that we should keep being filled with the Holy Spirit (Eph. 5:18). So, as the Holy Spirit falls upon us, the fruit of that should be the revelatory voice of God being spoken through the recipients of the Spirit.

- In Peter's inaugural sermon at Pentecost, he stated that the culmination of the New Covenant was wrapped up in a gift; namely, the gift of the Holy Spirit, and it was for children present and those to come, meaning all of us (Acts 2:38–39). This is actually a fulfillment of Isaiah's prophecy in Isaiah 59:21, which speaks quite specifically that the revelatory and prophetic word would never depart from our mouth. To stifle or shut out the revelatory voice of God or state that prophetic leadings, word of knowledge, or other Spirit-inspired gifts as no longer valid, as a cessationist would maintain, comes dangerously close to Jesus' warning about rejecting the Holy Spirit (Matt. 12:32).

In the final analysis a cessationist has very little biblical ground to walk on, so I would lovingly, but boldly encourage them to rethink their position in light of the Scripture. I might speak about the plethora of miracles that still take place today, citing recent polls of people witnessing God's miraculous power, including the miracles that I have witnessed myself. Finally, I truly like the closing words in Dr. Ruthven's book, and I would echo these to any cessationist: "If the Church has 'begun in the Spirit,' let us not attempt to change God's method to complete our course in the weakness of human flesh. Since it is the Father's good pleasure to 'give good gifts to them who ask Him,' it must be our pleasure to receive them humbly."

Appendix Two
Living in the Supernatural

—◦◦◦—

S ince 2008, I have been teaching the training course *Living in the Supernatural* (*LS*). This training material was written primarily out of desperation because I could not find anything like the content that is taught in this discipleship curriculum within the Holiness movement. Through this course, I have had the blessing of seeing many people embrace and experience the message of purity and power. What's more is that I'm constantly reminded through testimonies that many churches are still living in a supernatural culture. My calling is to re-dig the wells in the Holiness movement with the two-fold message of Word and Spirit, or purity and power. But more than that, I want *LS* to be more than merely another event for a church, I long to see churches sustain the move of God. My prayer is that this training material will help foster an ongoing environment where people replicate the life of Jesus every single day.

LS is still developing and probably will continue to evolve as it's taught in churches across the United States and beyond. As with any curriculum, it's not a panacea. But it's one of the few, in the Holiness movement, that uniquely fuses purity and power with a special emphasis on the supernatural gifts in 1 Corinthians 12:8–10. The training workbook contains nine lessons, which could be taught in eighteen to twenty hours or condensed for different applications. Generally, when I teach *LS* in churches, I teach four to six lessons in four evening services. Conferences afford the opportunity of day sessions, which allows for six sessions. Depending on the church and setting, different lessons will be taught out of the nine in the workbook. The six lessons that I feel are most pertinent are outlined here.

Lesson One: Understanding the Basics

This first lesson covers the challenges, opposition, and criticism Jesus experienced from the religious crowd, not to mention from his own family and townsmen, because of His display of miracles. Frankly, living like Jesus is costly, and the supernatural lifestyle often requires walking through challenges, persecutions, and great adversity. Not everyone will support a lifestyle that believes in the supernatural gifts. Jesus would have experienced few persecutions and insults had He not ventured into miracles. This lesson speaks about the necessity to emulate Jesus and His charismatic lifestyle, even when it becomes difficult. Additionally, I address the call given by Jesus to replicate His life given in the commission accounts. However, there is a necessity for holiness and heart purity if we are to sustain this charismatic lifestyle. The lesson usually ends with prayer, asking the Holy Spirit to give those present a Spirit of wisdom and revelation (Eph. 1:17) and for the participants to have a willingness to commit to this challenging lifestyle.

Lesson Two: Non-Negotiables

This lesson is extremely crucial because I address five components that are absolutely essential to sustain a supernatural lifestyle. I usually begin with an extensive teaching on sanctification and the necessity to live with a pure heart. Once the foundation of holiness has been built, I talk about the five non-negotiables. The five components are the following: the belief that God is always good, that signs point to a greater reality, that personal experiences cannot govern God's Word, that there needs to be a willingness to contend for breakthroughs, and that fruitful ministry always flows out of intimacy. The last of the five components, in my opinion, is the most essential. The class includes a discussion of the necessity to live like Mary at the feet of Jesus. Distractions deafen our ability to hear the Jesus' words, and therefore, we attempt to accomplish things for Him that He never requires. This class usually ends with prayer for recognition and repentance of the preoccupation and busyness that has become a distraction to hearing His voice.

Lesson Three: Where Did the Power Go?

This lesson gives a historical backdrop for the absence of power in the American church. I also cover how cessationism has crept into the Church during the rise of Hellenism and has divided Word and Spirit. We also look at various contemporary threats to the supernatural lifestyle including the overemphasis of preparation theology and the teachings by Benjamin Warfield who wrote *Counterfeit Miracles*. There is also an examination of the division of Word and Spirit that occurred in the early 1900s between the Holiness and Pentecostal churches, largely due to the Azusa Street Revival in 1906. This class is revelatory for Nazarenes because it shows historically how the denomination began and what possibilities exist when a church freely functions in purity and power. This class ends with prayer for the reuniting of purity and power.

Lesson Four: Fundamentals to Spiritual Gifts and How They Work

This lesson is the heart of *LS*. After laying a foundation for the necessity of character and holiness, posturing yourself at the feet of Jesus, and being willing to re-marry Word and Spirit, this lesson unpacks the supernatural gifts identified in 1 Corinthians 12:8–10. I try to spend adequate time giving a biblical context for the unique balance for character and *charismata* as given in 1 Corinthians chapters eleven through fourteen. I usually discuss how gifts are given, the purpose of the gifts, and the holy lifestyle that sustains them. Also, I talk about the importance of creating a culture of honor in the body of Christ along with the detriments of divisions, arrogance, and insecurity. The conclusion of this section examines each gift identified from its root meaning and how they are to be deployed with purpose and order. This class usually ends by asking the Holy Spirit to come and demonstrate Himself through the participants. We've often had people touched, healed, or delivered during this time.

Lesson Five: Creating a Prophetic Culture

This lesson unfolds the one spiritual gift that Paul said we should especially seek, the gift of prophecy (1 Cor. 14:1). I define prophecy and demonstrate how it is used in the Bible. Moreover, I underscore the fact that we must hear Jesus' words; therefore, we discuss the essential importance of having an uncluttered heart and life so that we're able to hear. This lesson also addresses the power of our words (see Prov. 18:21; Eph. 4:29), and it underscores the fact that life is contained in Jesus' words (see John 6:63). Therefore, speaking prophetically can instill life into the body of Christ.

There have been services when I will have people practice listening and speaking prophetically. They pair off together in groups, and spend time praying and listening and asking the Holy Spirit to speak about issues concerning their partners. They ask God to give them a Scripture, a phrase, or specific word believing that prophetic words edify, exhort, and comfort the body (1 Cor. 14:3). In almost every service where we practice this exercise, people are surprised at how freely the Holy Spirit desires to use them to build others up. God is more concerned about edifying His body than we are, so we simply need to become willing vessels. This is not something weird and fleshy; just simply the body ministering to the body through the power (guidance) of the Holy Spirit. Jesus spoke prophetically to the woman at the well (John 4:16–19). His words affected this woman's testimony that eventually changed an entire city (John 4:39). When believers speak prophetically, unbelievers' hearts may be revealed to the point that they repent and begin to worship God (1 Cor. 14:24–25). It is my desire to see churches become prophetic cultures where His Word is spoken. Life is in His voice; what could be better than speaking what He is saying to us?

Lesson Six: The More Excellent Way

The final lesson addresses the biblical definition of love. Paul called this kind of lifestyle the more excellent way (1 Cor. 12:31). This lesson takes us back to character-based living and the necessity to seek, embrace, and live in holiness. Gifts without character (love) are superfluous, and the Bible speaks directly to this issue. The creedal text that I usually start with is Jesus' words, "A new command I give you, that you love one another; as I have loved you, that you also love one another. By this all will know that you are My disciples, if you have love for one another" (John 13:34–35). The distinguishing characteristic of being Jesus' follower is found in the manner in which we love others. This verse expresses a profound, and certainly life-altering, statement that Jesus makes. In order to express divine love, we must first experience God's love; this usually sets up a time for experiencing a greater touch from God.

I normally conclude the last service with an impartation and activation. The impartations are simply prayer times in which we gather around the altar and we ask for an increase of the Holy Spirit in our lives. There is a small amount of teaching on this subject matter because this topic is not predominantly taught or understood in the Church of the Nazarene. Usually impartations are accompanied by the laying on of hands and praying for God's Spirit to bless, empower, and use the recipients with spiritual gifts.

God has been faithful over the years of teaching *LS*, and I've seen many churches come alive and walk in a supernatural culture. My deepest desire is to see churches and denominations live in the blessing of the Word and the Spirit working in conjunction with each other. The workbook that was written, *Living in the Supernatural,* is also a stand-alone resource that churches have purchased and used in their own small groups and discipleship experiences.

Recommended Reading

Billman, Frank H. *The Supernatural Thread in Methodism: Signs and Wonders Among Methodists Then and Now.* Lake Mary, FL: Creation House Press, 2013.

Brown, Candy Gunther. *Testing Prayer: Science and Healing.* Cambridge, Massachusetts: Harvard University Press, 2012.

Brown, Michael L. *Authentic Fire.* Lake Mary, FL: Creation House, 2015.

_____. *The Revival Answer Book.* Ventura, CA: Renew Books, 2001.

Bustin, G. T. *Dead: Yet... Live.* Westfield, Indiana: Fellowship Promoter Press, 1967.

Clark, Randy, ed. *Power, Holiness and Evangelism: Rediscovering God's Purity, Power, and Passion for the Lost.* Shippensburg, PA: Destiny Image Publishers, 1999.

_____, ed. *Supernatural Missions: The Impact of the Supernatural on World Missions.* Mechanicsburg, PA: Global Awakening, 2012.

_____. *There is More: The Secret to Experiencing God's Power to Change Your Life*. Minneapolis, MN: Chosen, 2013.

Cymbala, Jim. *Fresh Power: Experiencing the Vast Resources of the Spirit of God*. Grand Rapids, MI: Zondervan Publishing, 2001.

DeArteaga, William L. *Quenching the Spirit: Discover the Real Spirit Behind the Charismatic Controversy*. Lake Mary, FL: Creation House, 1996.

Dunn, James D. G. *Jesus and the Spirit*. Grand Rapids: Wm. B. Eerdmans Publishing Company, 1975.

Greig, Gary S., and Kevin N. Springer, eds. *The Kingdom and the Power*. Ventura, CA: Regal Books, 1993.

Hughey, Rhonda. *Desperate for His Presence: God's Design to Transform Your Life and Your City*. Bloomington, MN: Bethany House Publishers, 2004.

Jernigan, C. B. *Pioneer Days of the Holiness Movement in the Southwest*. Kansas City, MO: Nazarene Publishing House, 1919.

Keener, Craig S. *Miracles: The Credibility of The New Testament Accounts*. 2 vols. Grand Rapids, MI: Baker Academic, 2011.

Kinghorn, Kenneth Cain. *Gifts of the Spirit*. Nashville, TN: Abingdon Press, 1976.

Nathan, Rich, and Ken Wilson. *Empowered Evangelicals: Bringing Together the Best of the Evangelical and Charismatic Worlds*. Boise, ID: Ampelon Publishing, 2009.

Purkiser, W. T. *The Gifts of the Spirit.* Kansas City, MO: Beacon Hill Press, 1975.

Ruthven, Jon Mark. *On the Cessation of the Charismata: The Protestant Polemic on Post-Biblical Miracles.* Tulsa, OK: Word and Spirit Press, 1993, 2011.

_____. *What's Wrong with Protestant Theology: Traditional Theology Versus Biblical Emphasis.* Tulsa, OK: Word and Spirit Press, 2013.

Snyder, Howard A. *The Divided Flame: Wesleyans and The Charismatic Renewal.* Eugene, OR: WIPF and Stock, 1986.

Teykl, Terry. *The Presence Based Church.* Muncie, IN: Prayer Point Press, 2003.

Wagner, C. Peter. *This Changes Everything: How God Can Transform Your Mind and Change Your Life.* Ventura, CA: Regal Books, 2013.

Webster, Robert. *Methodism and the Miraculous: John Wesley's Idea of the Supernatural and the Identification of Methodists in the Eighteenth Century.* Lexington, KY: Emeth Press, 2013.

Living in the Supernatural

Living in the Supernatural is a stand-alone workbook that you can read at your own pace. It is filled with more than 475 Scriptures that explore the lifestyle that is normative for Spirit-filled believers. Learn why the present-day church has become fearful and suspect of the extraordinary power of the Holy Spirit, and what we can do to recover biblical expectations. Lessons include building the foundation of a supernatural lifestyle, how to use the spiritual gifts God gives in 1 Corinthians 12 to strengthen the body of Christ, and recognizing the fruits of functioning in the supernatural coming to life through you.

Begin a lifestyle in the supernatural as Jesus and the believers did in the New Testament.

Prevailing in the Battle Zone

Prevailing in the Battle Zone is also a stand-alone workbook designed to take you on a journey to spiritual freedom. With more than 525 Scriptures, you will understand the enemy's lies that keep your mind impregnated with hope-lessness, and you will chart a course to intimacy with Christ. By learning to recognize the ploys and tactics of the enemy you will gain insight on how to walk in spiritual victory every day. Lessons include understanding how to prevail in spiritual warfare, where the battle really is focused, identifying major strongholds, the keys to the kingdom, and walking in the freedom we have in Christ.

Founded by Rob McCorkle in 2008, Fire School Ministries has a specific vision of re-digging the wells in the Holiness movement uniting the message of purity and power (the Word and the Spirit). Our mission is to challenge pastors, leaders, and churches to replicate the ministry of Jesus and the primitive New Testament Church as witnessed in the book of Acts. We desire to train, equip, and impart a lifestyle that reproduces the supernatural work of Christ so that we can fulfill the Great Commission. Books and resources can be obtained by writing or emailing Fire School Ministries.

P.O. Box 511
Groveport, OH 43125
fireschoolministries@gmail.com
www.fireschoolministries.com

Endnotes

1   The Word ("Good News" or "Gospel") that Jesus preached was not merely creedal statements or a set of doctrinal statements that we adhere to, but prophetic utterance that brought people into an encounter with the Spirit of God. Therefore, when I speak about the Word, I'm hoping to expand your thinking beyond mere Bible knowledge and doctrinal content. Truly, the Word and the Spirit cannot be divided as we have erroneously done in the Protestant movement. The Word is always inclusive of the Spirit, and the Spirit is always inclusive of the Word.

2   *Living in the Supernatural* was written in 2008, primarily out of frustration that no such training program could be found within the Nazarene Church at the time, and will be discussed briefly in the appendix of this book. While many programs have been written within the denomination and provide many beneficial results, a discipleship program such as this particular one is rare. This material was the impetus behind my project—creating a self-replicating discipleship program that teaches purity and power in the Holiness movement. Since 2008, I've started a ministry organization called Fire School Ministries, dedicated to the message of Word and Spirit. From here after, *Living in the Supernatural* will be referred as (*LS*).

3   Jack Hayford, *A Passion for Fullness* (Fort Worth, TX: LIFE Publishing, 1990), 124.

4   These thoughts were inspired by Rich Nathan and Ken Wilson, *Empowered Evangelicals* (Boise, ID: Ampelon Publishing, 1995).

Rich's chapter, "Looking for the Best of Both Worlds," speaks directly to his understanding of uniting Word and Spirit.

5   Paul Cain and R. T. Kendall, *The Word and the Spirit: Reclaiming Your Covenant with the Holy Spirit and the Word of God* (Lake Mary, Florida: Creation House, 1998), xiv, xvii.

6   Mark Rutland, *The Finger of God: Reuniting Power and Holiness in the Church* (Wilmore, KY: Bristol Books, 1988), 10.

7   Gordon Fee, *God's Empowering Presence* (Grand Rapids, MI: Baker Academic, 1994), 35.

8   See James D. G. Dunn, *Jesus and the Spirit* (Grand Rapids, MI: Wm. B. Eerdmans Publishing Company, 1975), 87; W. T. Purkiser, *The Gifts of the Spirit* (Kansas City, MO: Beacon Hill Press, 1975), 17. Purkiser was a prominent writer in the Church of the Nazarene, and here he writes, "In the New Testament use of the term, all Christians are charismatic." For a fuller description, see Howard Snyder, *The Divided Flame: Wesleyans & The Charismatic Renewal* (Eugene, OR: WIPF & Stock, 1986), 11–18.

9   Ramsay MacMullen, *Christianizing the Roman Empire A.D. 100–400* (New Haven: Yale University Press, 1984), 26.

10   Randy Clark, ed., *Supernatural Mission: The Impact of the Supernatural on World Mission* (Mechanicsburg, PA: Global Awakening, 2012), 17.

11   Warren Wiersbe, ed., *The Best of A.W. Tozer* (Camp Hill, PA: Wing Spread Publishers, 2007), 145.

12   Jim Cymbala, *Fresh Power* (Grand Rapids, MI: Zondervan Publishing House, 2001), 48.

13   Jack Deere, *Surprised by the Voice of God* (Grand Rapids, MI: Zondervan Publishing House, 1996), 358.

14   John Wesley, *The Works of John Wesley* (Kansas City, MO: Beacon Hill Press, 1986), 1:170.

15   Michael L. Brown, *The Revival Answer Book* (Ventura, CA: Renew Books, 2001), 15.

16   Craig S. Keener, *Miracles: The Credibility of the New Testament Accounts* (Grand Rapids, MI: Baker Academics, 2011), 1:383.

17   Wesley, *The Works,* 8:465.

18 Wesley, *The Works,* 7:27.

19 Jon Mark Ruthven, *What's Wrong with Protestant Theology: Traditional Theology Verses Biblical Emphasis* (Tulsa, OK: Word and Spirit Press, 2013), 211. This quote is actually from the pre-published manuscript. When this book was published, the editors took this particular statement out of the book. It is rather unfortunate because it makes the point very well.

20 Keith Drury, "The Holiness Movement: Dead or Alive?" http://www.crivoice.org/copyright.html (accessed March 15, 2011).

21 "The Holiness Manifesto," http://www.christianitytoday.com/ct/2006/marchweb-only/113-13.0.html (accessed March 12, 2011).

22 Jon Mark Ruthven, *On the Cessation of the Charismata: The Protestant Polemic on Post-Biblical Miracles* (Tulsa, OK: Word and Spirit Press, 1993, 2011), 171. See Snyder, *The Divided Flame,* 22–27. Snyder talks about how the Church quickly drifted toward institutionalization after the first few centuries, which had a negative effect on the Holy Spirit and spiritual gifts. The freedom of the Holy Spirit was quickly replaced by decorum, liturgy, and ritualism, all of which created fuel for cessationism.

23 Fred and Sharon Wright, *The World's Greatest Revivals* (Shippensburg, PA: Destiny Image Publishers, 2007), 81.

24 William DeArteaga, *Quenching the Spirit* (Lake Mary, FL: Creation House, 1992), 71.

25 Frank H. Billman, *The Supernatural Thread in Methodism: Signs and Wonders Among Methodists Then and Now* (Lake Mary, FL: Creation House Press, 2013), 10.

26 Ruthven, *Cessation of the Charismata,* 19.

27 Ibid., 21. It should be noted that both, Augustine and Aquinas, had charismatic experiences later in life and refuted their earlier teachings.

28 Eddie Hyatt, *2000 Years of Charismatic Christianity* (Lake Mary, FL: Charisma House, 2002), 76.

29 Ruthven, *Cessationism of the Charismata,* 22. Cessationism became the official state position for a time during the Interregnum of Oliver Cromwell, as it was enshrined in the very first paragraph of the

Westminster Confession of Faith (1646)—a creed that was to be imposed on all of the British Isles by force. It held that all revelation had been confined to the Bible, and therefore, there is no need for the Spirit to speak prophetic utterances.

30 Ibid., 24.

31 Keener, *Miracles: The Credibility,* 1:118.

32 Ruthven, *Cessation of the Charismata,* 28.

33 Wesley, *The Works,* 10:1–79.

34 Robert Webster, *Methodism and the Miraculous* (Lexington, KY: Emeth Press, 2013), 11.

35 Wesley, *The Works,* 1:189.

36 Billman, *The Supernatural Thread,* 30.

37 Henry D. Rack, *Reasonable Enthusiast: John Wesley and the Rise of Methodism* (London: Epworth Press, 2002), 275–276.

38 Rack, *Reasonable Enthusiast,* 276.

39 Steve Beard, *Thunderstruck: John Wesley and the Toronto Blessing* (Wilmore, KY: Thunderstruck Communications, 1996), 3.

40 Rack, *Reasonable Enthusiast,* 276.

41 John Telford, ed., *The Letters of John Wesley* (London: The Epworth Press, 1931), 303.

42 This is from an unpublished work that our class was privileged to read. William L. De Arteaga, *Forging a Renewed Hebraic and Pauline Christianity,* 187. Frank Billman describes how Allen asked to be prayed for following his sanctification experience. Although the prayer group was reluctant at first, they followed the mandate of Mark 16:17–18. See Billman, *Supernatural Thread,* 46.

43 De Arteaga, *Renewed Hebraic and Pauline Christianity,* 184.

44 Palmer promoted belief in divine healing throughout the Holiness movement, too. See Keener, *Miracles: The Credibility,* 1:392.

45 De Arteaga, *Renewed Hebraic and Pauline Christianity,* 190. Cullis was also motivated toward a healing ministry after he prayed for a patient of his with a brain tumor and she was healed. See Keener, *Miracles: The Credibility of The New Testament Accounts,* 1:391.

46 Ibid., 194.

47 Billman, *Supernatural Thread,* 69.

48   Laurence W. Wood, *The Meaning of Pentecost in Early Methodism: Rediscovering John Fletcher as John Wesley's Vindicator and Designated Successor* (Lantham, MD: Scarecrow Press, 2002), 332.

49   Kenneth Scott Latourette, *A History of Christianity: Reformation to the Present* (New York, NY: Harper & Row Publishers, 1953, 1975), 2:1419.

50   Latourette, *A History of Christianity*, 2:1420.

51   Wood, *The Meaning of Pentecost*, 332.

52   Billman, *Supernatural Thread*, 70

53   De Arteaga, *Quenching the Spirit*, 130.

54   Billman, *Supernatural Thread*, 70.

55   Ruthven, *Cessation of the Charismata*, 58.

56   Ibid., 62.

57   Hyatt, *2000 Years*, 76.

58   In all this, Warfield, of course, was defending the infamous paragraph 1 of the Westminster Confession of Faith (1647), the theological tradition to which he was thoroughly committed.

59   Ruthven, *Cessationism of the Charismata*, 90

60   Ibid., 57. There were other suspicions concerning miracles lurking in the minds of people during this period of time too, including a reaction to Catholic relics. See Keener, *Miracles: The Credibility*, 1:371–377.

61   Latourette, *History of Christianity*, 2:1420–1421.

62   Ruthven, *Cessationism of the Charismata*, 37.

63   Vinson Synan, *The Century of the Holy Spirit: 100 years of Pentecostal and Charismatic Renewal* (Nashville, TN:Thomas Nelson, 2001), 15.

64   Synan, *The Century of the Holy Spirit*, 41.

65   Ibid., 42.

66   Ibid., 49.

67   Stephen A. Seamands, "The Great Divorce: How Power and Purity Got Separated." In Randy Clark, ed., *Power, Holiness and Evangelism* (Shippensburg, PA: Destiny Image Publishers, 1999), 121.

68   Synan, *The Century of the Holy Spirit*, 204.

69 Wright, *Greatest Revivals*, 176.

70 Synan, *The Century of the Holy Spirit*, 204.

71 Ibid., 203.

72 Ibid., 204.

73 Ibid.

74 Kenneth Cain Kinghorn, *Gifts of the Spirit* (Nashville, TN: Abingdon Press, 1976), 19.

75 H. Orton Wiley and Paul T. Culbertson, *Introduction to Christian Theology* (Kansas City, MO: Beacon Hill Press, 1945), 49.

76 H. Ray Dunning, *Grace, Faith, and Holiness* (Kansas City, MO: Beacon Hill Press, 1988), 93.

77 James D. G. Dunn, *New Testament Theology: An Introduction* (Nashville, TN: Abingdon Press, 2009), 159.

78 Fee, *God's Empowering Presence*, 2.

79 J. Kenneth Grider, *A Wesleyan-Holiness Theology* (Kansas City, MO: Beacon Hill Press, 1994), 32–34.

80 Mark W. Pfeifer, *Alignment: A Blueprint for the 21st Century Church* (Kearney, NE: Morris Publishing, 2008), 53–54.

81 DeArteaga, *Forging a Renewed Hebraic and Pauline Christianity*, 207.

82 Michael L. Brown, *The Revival Answer Book* (Ventura, CA: Renew Books, 2001), 7. It might be noted that Brown says very few people know, or even recognize, the names of John Wesley's critics. Yet, most people know who Wesley is. The point is, in the grand scheme, people will remember the revivalists but fail to remember who their critics are. True revivalists make an impact in people's lives; they make a transformational difference for God in their world. Critics, on the other hand, rarely make a difference in their world for the kingdom of God. Consequently, they are scarcely remembered.

83 Ibid., 16.

84 Ruthven, *What's Wrong*, 27.

85 Ibid., 260.

86 Ibid., 35.

87 James D. G. Dunn, *Jesus, Paul, and the Gospels* (Grand Rapids, MI: Eerdmans Publishing Co., 2011), 109.

88 Ruthven, *What's Wrong*, 203.
89 Dunn, *Jesus, Paul, and the Gospels*, 177–180.
90 Ibid., 258.
91 H. Seebass, "Holy," in *The New International Dictionary of New Testament Theology*, ed. Colin Brown (Grand Rapids, MI: Zondervan Publishing House, 1976), 2:232. Referred to *NIDNTT* hereafter.
92 Ibid., 2:230.
93 Ruthven, *What's Wrong*, 245, 249.
94 Ibid., 256, 258.
95 Ibid., 265.
96 Ibid., 29.
97 Gary S. Greig and Kevin N. Springer, eds., *The Kingdom and the Power* (Ventura, CA: Regal Books, 1993), 176-178.
98 Ray VanderLaan, *Echoes of His Presence* (Grand Rapids, MI: Zondervan Publishing House, 1996), 59.
99 Ruthven, *What's Wrong*, 246.
100 Summary statements concerning Jesus' ministry, healing and exorcisms: Matt. 4:15; 4:23; 8:18; 9:35; 14:14; 15:30–31; 19:2; 21:14; Mark 1:34; 3:10; Luke 4:18; 4:40–41; 5:15; 6:19; 7:21; 9:11; 13:33. Many of these same verses are cited in Ruthven, *What's Wrong*, 247.
101 Ibid., 248.
102 Ibid., 249.
103 Seabass, "Holy," *NIDNTT*, 2:231.
104 DeArteaga, *Forging a Renewed Hebraic and Pauline Christianity*, 452.
105 Ibid.
106 Seamands, "The Great Divorce: How Power and Purity Got Separated," 121–132.
107 Ibid., 131–132.
108 Ibid., 132.
109 G. T. Bustin, *Dead: Yet ... Live* (Westfield, Indiana: Fellowship Promoter Press, 1967). See also G.T Bustin, *The Man Christ Jesus* (Salem, OH: Schmul Publishing Co., Inc, 1987). Schmul Publishers reprint old classics; Bustin wrote this book in the late 1960s.

110 Ibid., 20.

111 Ruthven, *Cessation of the Charismata,* 169.

112 Ibid.

113 Bill Johnson, *Face to Face with God: The Ultimate Quest to Experience His Presence* (Lake Mary, Florida: Charisma House, 2007), 189.

114 Hayford, *A Passion for Fullness,* 113.

115 James D. G. Dunn, "Romans 1–8," in *Word Biblical Commentary,* ed. Bruce M. Metzger, vol. 38A (Waco, TX: Word Publishers, 1988), lxxi.

116 J. Lee Grady, *The Holy Spirit is Not for Sale: Rekindling the Power of God in an Age of Compromise* (Grand Rapids, MI: Chosen Books, 2010), 26.

117 Ibid., 91.

118 DeArteaga, *Forging a Renewed Hebraic and Pauline Christianity,* 413.

119 Ibid., 414.

120 *Manual, Church of the Nazarene 2009–2013* (Kansas City, MO: Nazarene Publishing House, 2009), 37.

121 James D. G. Dunn, *Jesus and the Spirit: A Study of the Religious and Charismatic Experiences of Jesus and the First Christians as Reflected in the New Testament* (Grand Rapids, MI: William B. Eerdmans Publishing Company, 1975), 88.

122 Bill Johnson and Randy Clark, *The Essential Guide to Healing: Equipping All Christians to Pray for the Sick* (Minneapolis, MN: Chosen Books, 2011), 80.

123 H. Orton Wiley, *Christian Theology* (Kansas City, MO: Beacon Hill Press, 1943), 2:321.

124 Gordon Fee, "The First Epistle to the Corinthians," in *The New International Commentary on the New Testament* (Grand Rapids, MI: William B. Eerdmans Publishing Company, 1987), 589.

125 For a great historical backdrop to Ephesus and an understanding of miracles see Rick Renner, *Light in the Darkness,* vol. 1 (Tulsa, OK: Teach All Nations, 2010).

126 Donald Metz, "1 Corinthians," in *Beacon Bible Commentary,* ed. A. F. Harper, W. M. Greathouse, Ralph Earle and W. T. Purkiser (Kansas City, MO: Beacon Hill Press, 1968, 1970) 8:446.

127 Ibid., 8:455

128 Dick Howard, *Tongues Speaking in the New Testament* (Norwalk, ME: Western Main Graphic Publication, 1980) 65–66. Howard's book is one of the most biblically inductive and objective examinations of the subject of tongues, especially for Nazarenes. However, his conclusion at the end of the book concerning the *charismata* is sympathetic to cessationism.

129 C. B. Jernigan, *Pioneer Days of the Holiness Movement in the Southwest* (Kansas City, MO: Nazarene Publishing House, 1919), 45.

130 Ruthven, *What's Wrong,* 83–84.

131 Ibid., 84.

132 For an interesting description of this word *kerux,* see Rick Renner, *Sparkling Gems from the Greek* (Tulsa, OK: Teach All Nations, 2003), 469–471.

133 Bob Sorge, *The Fire of Delayed Answers* (Greenwood, MO: Oasis House, 1996), 219.

134 Bob Sorge, *Pain, Perplexity, and Promotion* (Greenwood, MO: Oasis House, 1999), 176.

135 James L. Garlow, *The Covenant* (Kansas City, MO: Beacon Hill Press, 1999), 37.

136 Dunn, *Jesus and the Spirit,* 202–203.

137 C. S. Lewis, *The Screwtape Letters* (Westwood, NJ: Barbour Books, 1990), 47.

138 Renner, *Sparkling Gems,* 525–526.

CPSIA information can be obtained
at www.ICGtesting.com
Printed in the USA
LVOW13s0330211216
518165LV00001B/1/P